JOB SEARCH
Secrets

JOB SEARCH
Secrets

Don Lussier with Tom Noteman
Edited by Donna M. Henderson

VGM Career Horizons
NTC/Contemporary Publishing Company

Library of Congress Cataloging-in-Publication Data

Lussier, Donald E.
    Job search secrets / Don Lussier with Tom Noteman ; edited by
Donna M. Henderson.
       p.   cm.
    ISBN 0-8442-4473-2
    1. Job Hunting.   2. Résumés (Employment)   I. Noteman,
Tom. II. Henderson, Donna M. III. Title.
HF5382.7.L873   1997
650.14—dc21   97-15803
                                                  CIP

Cover design by Monica Baziuk
Interior design and production by City Desktop Productions, Inc.

Published by VGM Career Horizons
An imprint of NTC/Contemporary Publishing Company
4255 West Touhy Avenue, Lincolnwood (Chicago), Illinois 60646-1975 U.S.A.
Copyright © 1998 by NTC/Contemporary Publishing Company
Printed in the United States of America
International Standard Book Number: 0-8442-4473-2
  15   14   13   12   11   10   9   8   7   6   5   4   3   2   1

Author Don Lussier passed away before this book went to print. As his daughter and editor I dedicate *Job Search Secrets* to him—for all his genius, creativity and passion for life—and to Mom, his "Honey"—for her love, sacrifice, and support. Thank you for the true love lesson.

Donna M. Henderson

Contents

Preface

Don Lussier helped numerous people "find their way" to new
employment opportunities. These people came from a wide
range of careers and industries. Don was well respected by
the people he counseled over the years and earned the admiration
of his peers. He continuously strived to perfect his craft and share
"what worked." I believe this book represents a distillation of the
knowledge and experience which Don learned and perfected during
his years as a Job Counselor and Advisor.

I met Don when we were both working at the same firm. Over
the five year period we worked together, we had many professional
discussions about the job search process and "what worked, and
what didn't work." In most areas we wholeheartedly agreed with
each other; however, there were a few areas in which we had our
own ideas. One such area is Chapter 2, in which Don suggests stay-
ing away from the Human Resources Department, unless you are
looking for a job in Human Resources. Being a Human Resources
professional, I take exception to that approach. However, you will
have to make up your own mind.

During the period Don and I worked together and afterward,
we developed a very special friendship. Don had written this book,
but prior to it being published, his days were cut short by his

untimely death. Don's family graciously asked me to help bring this book to fruition. I truly believe that *Job Search Secrets* is a book that will provide you with many useful, practical, and insightful approaches to your job search. You can SOAR!!

Tom Noteman

About the Authors

Don Lussier

Author of five other job search books, Don Lussier had over a decade of job search counseling and instruction experience. He was the cofounder of the first Michigan-based outplacement firm, and he conducted job search counseling and training for well over one hundred and fifty companies, organizations, and schools across the United States and Canada. He counseled individuals and groups of all types and at all levels including: college graduates, professionals, blue-collar workers, managers, and educators.

Mr. Lussier lived in Orion, Michigan, with his wife, Loretta. They have three children, Patty, Donna, and Scott, and eight grandchildren who affectionately refer to him as "Bubba."

Thomas (Tom) J. Noteman

Tom Noteman's career in Human Resources has spanned thirty years. As a Human Resources "practitioner" he has recruited employees for all levels within organizations. Starting in Detroit, his career took him to Des Moines, Iowa; Racine, Wisconsin; Toronto, Ontario; Toledo, Ohio; and back to Detroit. During a five year period, he worked as a Job Counselor assisting and advising candidates on managing their careers, developing their job search skills, and locating new job opportunities. In 1990, Tom returned to being a Human Resources practitioner, as Director, Human Resources for a multinational company. Tom has been married to his wife, Judy, for almost thirty-five years and has three grown children. He earned his degree in English Literature from Wayne State University in Detroit.

Chapter 1

How to Leave the Competition in the Dust

W ant a great new job? It all starts here.

If you think that writing your resume is the toughest thing you have to do associated with your job search, think again. After you complete this self-inventory, writing your resume will be a piece of cake. This is where the rubber meets the road. If you think that you can skip over or pay little regard to these exercises, don't even bother looking for a new position.

After nearly 15 years as an outplacement consultant and author I have arrived at one definite conclusion: *people with low self-esteem or self-worth make terrible job seekers.* When I meet candidates for the first time there is one thing I immediately look for: how do they feel about their value to an employer?

I don't care if they are ticked off at the employer for letting them go. (Actually, I do care, but that's beside the point I wish to make here.) If I discover the candidates do not feel good about what they have to offer lucky employers, I know the road ahead will be long and rocky.

1

That is precisely why I have worked so hard to develop an exhaustive series of self-inventory exercises—to show you that you do have some good "stuff" to offer an employer. In all likelihood, you have forgotten nearly all of the wonderful things you have done for past employers. You need the thoroughness of these exercises to bring all of these important personal assets and experiences back to mind. Most of us are too busy working to recall all of the things we have done in the past.

Once you begin to discover how much you're really worth, you'll actually look forward to writing your resume, creating great cover letters, and landing and having great interviews. Once you believe in yourself, it's a whole lot easier to get others to believe in you also.

Personal Attributes Inventory

Everyone knows that employers are looking for experience, skills, and accomplishments. Few job seekers stop to think how important their personal work habits or attributes are. Because most of your competition will fail to sell themselves in this area, you should make it a point to do so.

Think about it: if you were hiring someone and you had two candidates with equal experience and skills, which one would you choose? Probably the one you think would be the best to work with day in and day out, the one displaying the most positive personal attributes— enthusiasm, dependability, adaptability, initiative, and so on.

This personal attributes inventory should be completed in three steps:

1. Go through the lists placing a check mark next to those attributes you feel you possess.
2. Go back to the first of the words you have checked off. Ask yourself, if I were doing the hiring, which of the attributes I just checked off would impress me the most? Place a second check mark next to these.
3. Move on to the attribute and validation portion of this exercise. Under the attribute column, record each of the double-checked words. Under the validation column, alongside each attribute, write a validating statement—a specific statement that proves that what you claim to be, you are.

EXAMPLE:

Attribute	Validation
dependable	*missed three days work in two years*
loyal	*stayed with the company until it closed its doors*
initiative	*initiated publication of company newsletter*
hard worker	*assumed purchaser's responsibilities upon reduction*

Whatever personal attribute you claim, it is imperative that you immediately make a validating statement showing you are not just exaggerating your own merits. As mentioned in the opening paragraph, your competition will almost always neglect to sell themselves in this area. The few who do will likely fail to immediately offer a specific statement proving that what they claim is true. Here then, is a great way to gain an immediate competitive edge.

PERSONAL ATTRIBUTES INVENTORY

Attribute	Validation
achiever	Worked my way up quickly (MGR in 3 yrs) · learned tee-lok program in less than 6 months
active	Always Moving –
adaptable	Successfully Operated in several market areas + different type of companies
aggressive	
ambitious	Sincere Desire to succeed
analytical	
assertive	
astute	
attentive	
bold	
calculating	
congenial	very easy to talk to / polite
conscientious	Always Empathetic to customer needs

Like to pride myself on

consistent Always Being Punctual

coordinator Coordinate tasks within Engineering Dept. / Sales / production

creative _____

decision maker – Can make clear Decisions quickly based on information presented

efficient Consistently Handled multiple projects Able to prioritize

energetic Dont like to be idle – worked 35 hrs/wk while @ college full time
60+ hrs as mgr @ 84

enterprising _____

exacting _____

flexible Like a chameleon Dealt with unsophisticated subs to very Professional volume Bul

friendly Always get Along w/ people – Many compliments from customers

forceful _____

forward thinking Have clear career goals set (goal oriented)
continually strive to improve systems in place

good follow-through _____

good-natured _____

hard-working worked 50+ hrs/wk for 6 years

honest Like to pride myself on Being honest

imaginative _____

independent Had P+L responsibilities @ 84 Freedom to get there However I wanted
Able to research independently + come up w/ answers

industrious _____

intelligent _____

persevering _____

persistent _____

personable _____

planner Very goal oriented

positive Good Attitude, strong work ethic

pragmatic _____

pride in appearance _____

problem solver _Able to overcome scheduling/logistic problems_

productive _Handled sales volume of 1 mill.+ while acting as_
proficient _support for outside sales + customer service_

profit oriented _____

punctual _Always 15 min. Early_

quick learner _Quickly moved through projects training o_
+ 84 training _Dealingers_
realistic _____

reliable _15 min Early - Strong work Ethic - SO.LAST_
6 yrs
resourceful _figured out Alternative products_

self-reliant _____

self-starter _____

systematic _____

tactful _____

works well alone _always met sales goals w/no_
Supervision

Skills, Action Words, Duties, and Responsibilities

Skills, action words, duties, and responsibilities—these are the words that gain attention, denote action, and invigorate statements. The following words can propel you to the head of the job-hunting pack:

devised–reinforced–persuaded–implemented–generated

Too many job seekers use the same three or four words or phrases over and over again, "I supervised this . . . I supervised that . . . I supervised this other thing." Personal pronouns have no place in a resume. A resume is a business document, not an autobiography. Phrases such as those just cited should thus become "Supervised this . . . supervised that . . . supervised this other thing."

The repeated use of the same word, such as "supervised," can, however, quickly induce boredom. For this reason you must look for appropriate synonyms. For example: *"Supervised* this . . . *directed* that . . . *managed* this other thing."

There are a number of ways to assemble an inventory of all of your saleable assets. One way is to simply recall the things that you did in past positions. Another better method is to review each position mentally as to what you did in a normal day's work. First you did this, then you did that, and so on. In doing so, you should try to recall the people you worked with and for, the results of these alliances, and the things, processes, tools, and equipment with which you are familiar.

There is yet another and more thorough way to approach this all important self-inventory. That is to break your work history into three areas: *People, Things,* and *Data.*

Most of us have more experience in one of these three areas than in the other two. You should begin your inventory in the area where you have the greatest amount of experience. Then, after having thoroughly exhausted this area, turn to the next and finally to the last. Although the bulk of your experience will probably lie in one area, you undoubtedly have had some excellent experiences in the other two areas as well.

In order to maximize the results of this inventory, I have included just about every action word or duty and responsibility possible. You will soon see that the great majority of these words have little to do with your background. You will also discover the same word or words often appear under more than one category. Don't let this put you off. Keep plugging away at it until you reach the end.

Be forewarned: this is not an exercise you can do between dinner and the evening news. You should expect to spend as many as two or three hours completing it. You might even like to do it in two or three sessions in order to maintain your mental alertness. So be it. Just be certain you don't skimp, give it short shrift, or try to avoid it altogether.

presented training materials to staff every sat. at 84

PEOPLE

Descriptive Statement(s)
addressed — *interviewers + code personell & response*
administered —

advised _MTS + G mgrs @ 84_

analyzed _Balance sheets sales records @ 84_   _Determined stocking levels for Commodities bought number based on_

appointed _hired part time employees_

appraised _____

arbitrated _Between employee disputes_

assessed _____

assisted _sales in any product knowledge area_

awarded _____

bargained _with suppliers/customers to negotiate best possible_

coached _employees to reach sales goals - become more knowledgeable_

communicated _with all levels of mgmt employees_

conferred _____

consolidated _tasks w/in UFP engineering dept_

consulted _____

contracted _____

coordinated _____

corrected _____

counseled _____

delegated _Tasks to Salesmen_

directed _____

disciplined _84_

educated _84_

eliminated _____

employed _____

enforced _____

enlisted _____

enrolled _____

evaluated _____

explained _____

fostered _____

governed _____

graded _____

handled _____

hired _____

influenced _____

instructed _____

interfaced _____

interviewed _____

introduced _____

issued _____

judged _____

lectured _____

led _____

managed _____

manipulated _____

matched _____

measured _____

mediated _____

monitored _____

motivated _____

negotiated _____

nominated _____

observed _____

organized _____

persuaded _____

prepared _____

promoted _____

qualified _____

questioned _____

recommended _____

reconciled _____

recruited _____

reduced _____

referred _____

rehabilitated _____

reported _____

represented _____

resolved _____

reviewed _____

scheduled _____

selected _____

served _____

showed _____

supervised _____

supported _____

taught _____

tested _____

trained _____

tutored _____

unified _____

united _____

verified _____

THINGS

Descriptive Statement(s)

acquired _____

activated _____

adapted _____

addressed _____

adopted _____

advertised _____

analyzed _____

appointed _____

appraised _____

approved _____

arbitrated _____

arranged _____

ascertained _____

assembled _____

assessed _____

assisted _____

attained _____

audited _____

averted _____

awarded _____

balanced _____

budgeted _____

built _____

calculated _____

cataloged _____

centralized _____

charted _____

checked _____

classified _____

collaborated _____

collected _____

combined _____

communicated _____

compared _____

compiled _____

completed _____

composed _____

computed _____

conceived _____

conceptualized _____

condensed _____

conducted _____

conferred _____

connected _____

conserved _____

consolidated _____

constructed _____

consulted _____

contracted _____

controlled _____

converted _____

coordinated _____

corrected _____

correlated _____

created _____

cycled _____

decided _____

decreased _____

defined _____

delivered _____

demonstrated _____

designed _____

detailed _____

detected _____

determined _____

developed _____

devised _____

diagnosed _____

directed _____

discovered _____

dispensed _____

displayed _____

distributed _____

diverted _____

documented _____

doubled _____

drafted _____

dramatized _____

established _____

estimated _____

evaluated _____

examined _____

expanded _____

expedited _____

experimented _____

explained _____

extended _____

extracted _____

fabricated _____

facilitated _____

fed _____

finalized _____

financed _____

forecast _____

formed _____

formulated _____

fostered _____

found _____

founded _____

furnished _____

generated _____

grouped _____

guaranteed _____

guided _____

handled _____

helped _____

hypothesized _____

identified _____

illustrated _____

implemented _____

improved _____

improvised _____

increased _____

indexed _____

influenced _____

informed _____

initiated _____

innovated _____

inspected _____

installed _____

instituted _____

instructed _____

integrated _____

interpreted _____

introduced _____

invented _____

inventoried _____

invested _____

investigated _____

issued _____

judged _____

launched _____

learned _____

liquidated _____

logged _____

made _____

maintained _____

managed _____

manipulated _____

mapped _____

marketed _____

matched _____

measured _____

modeled _____

modernized _____

modified _____

monitored _____

navigated _____

negotiated _____

observed _____

obtained _____

offered _____

opened _____

operated _____

ordered _____

organized _____

originated _____

oversaw _____

painted _____

perceived _____

performed _____

persuaded _____

photographed _____

piloted _____

pinpointed _____

pioneered _____

planned _____

predicted _____

prepared _____

prescribed _____

presented _____

prevented _____

processed _____

procured _____

programmed _____

projected _____

promoted _____

proposed _____

protected _____

proved _____

provided _____

publicized _____

published _____

purchased _____

qualified _____

quantified _____

raised _____

read _____

realized _____

received _____

recommended _____

reconciled _____

reconstructed _____

recorded _____

rectified _____

redesigned _____

reduced _____

referred _____

refined _____

rehabilitated _____

reinforced _____

related _____

rendered _____

reorganized _____

reported _____

represented _____

researched _____

resolved _____

responded _____

restored _____

restructured _____

retrieved _____

reviewed _____

revised _____

revitalized _____

salvaged _____

satisfied _____

scheduled _____

secured _____

selected _____

separated _____

served _____

serviced _____

set up _____

shaped _____

shared _____

showed _____

simplified _____

sketched _____

sold _____

solved _____

sorted _____

standardized _____

streamlined _____

structured _____

studied _____

submitted _____

substantiated _____

supervised _____

supplemented _____

supplied _____

surveyed _____

synthesized _____

systematized _____

tabulated _____

tailored _____

taught _____

tended _____

tested _____

tooled _____

trained _____

transacted _____

transcribed _____

translated _____

traveled _____

treated _____

uncovered _____

undertook _____

unified _____

united _____

updated _____

upgraded _____

used _____

verified _____

weighed _____

wired _____

worked _____

wrote _____

DATA

Descriptive Statement(s)

accumulated _____

acquired _____

adapted _____

analyzed _____

appraised _____

arranged _____

ascertained _____

assembled _____

assessed _____

audited _____

balanced _____

calculated _____

cataloged _____

categorized _____

charted _____

checked _____

classified _____

collected _____

combined _____

communicated _____

compared _____

compiled _____

completed _____

composed _____

computed _____

computerized _____

conceived _____

consolidated _____

converted _____

coordinated _____

copied _____

corrected _____

correlated _____

created _____

decided _____

delivered _____

designed _____

detailed _____

detected _____

determined _____

developed _____

diagnosed _____

directed _____

discovered _____

dispensed _____

displayed _____

distributed _____

diverted _____

documented _____

drafted _____

edited _____

ensured _____

entered _____

established _____

estimated _____

evaluated _____

examined _____

exchanged _____

expanded _____

expedited _____

experimented _____

explained _____

extracted _____

facilitated _____

filed _____

finalized _____

forecast _____

formulated _____

found _____

furnished _____

gathered _____

generated _____

grouped _____

guaranteed _____

handled _____

helped _____

hypothesized _____

identified _____

illustrated _____

implemented _____

improvised _____

indexed _____

initiated _____

inspected _____

installed _____

instituted _____

interpreted _____

introduced _____

invented _____

inventoried _____

investigated _____

issued _____

launched _____

learned _____

logged _____

made _____

mailed _____

maintained _____

managed _____

manipulated _____

mapped _____

matched _____

measured _____

modified _____

monitored _____

observed _____

obtained _____

ordered _____

organized _____

originated _____

oversaw _____

packaged _____

perceived _____

performed _____

pinpointed _____

posted _____

predicted _____

prepared _____

prescribed _____

presented _____

prevented _____

printed _____

prioritized _____

processed _____

procured _____

produced _____

programmed _____

projected _____

protected _____

proved _____

provided _____

publicized _____

published _____

qualified _____

quantified _____

questioned _____

read _____

received _____

recommended _____

reconciled _____

reconstructed _____

reduced _____

researched _____

resolved _____

restored _____

retrieved _____

reviewed _____

revised _____

saved _____

scheduled _____

secured _____

selected _____

separated _____

showed _____

simplified _____

sold _____

sorted _____

standardized _____

stored _____

streamlined _____

structured _____

studied _____

submitted _____

supplemented _____

supplied _____

surveyed _____

systematized _____

tabulated _____

tailored _____

tracked _____

transcribed _____

transferred _____

translated _____

used _____

verified _____

wrote _____

Accomplishments and Achievements

Employers love accomplishments and achievements. The more you can tell them about *and prove* the more they will like you. If your background provided you with the opportunity to do something extra, to rise above the crowd, to perform with excellence now is the time to get it in writing.

This exercise is designed to make it as painless as possible to recall and record your on-the-job achievements. Use it as a memory activator. It is not meant to be all-inclusive. You might very well have achieved some things not included in this list. Completing this inventory will help you remember some of those things.

The inventory is divided into three sections, each prefaced by a capital letter.

For example:

A—Achieved, Exceeded, Improved, Increased

Beneath each section is a category heading:

Production

Beneath each category head is a list of possible areas of accomplishment:

Accuracy _____

Capacity _____

Efficiency _____

Directions: Check off those areas in which you have accomplishments. Then, next to each accomplishment, write a brief statement telling about it.

Examples:

Efficiency   *Increased operating efficiency 25 percent—saving $122,000 in 1995.*

Initiated   *Introduced data-based sales and marketing program reducing double mailings by 18% and saving company $75,000 in postage in 1996.*

Take your time. Be thorough. Use more paper if necessary. How much time you devote to this inventory will directly affect how much time it will take you to win (or not win) a job you qualify for and want.

Be certain to use quantifiers (dollars, numbers, and percentages) whenever possible. If you have to guesstimate, do so, but be certain to stay on the conservative side of the ledger. If you saved $5 an hour that's $40 in an eight hour day, times five days in a week = $200 per week, times 52 weeks in a year = $10,400 per year!

INVENTORY

A—Achieved, Exceeded, Improved, Increased . . .

Production

Accuracy _____

Capacity _____

Controls _____

Efficiency _____

Gross _____

Inventory _____

Margin _____

Operating income _____

Performance _____

Product quality/reliability _____

Product rating _____

Production controls _____

Production goals/quotas _____

Productivity _____

Profitability _____

Quality _____

Safety _____

Standards _____

Utilization _____

Volume _____

Sales/Marketing/Service

Customer base _____

Customer satisfaction _____

Customer service _____

Market share/penetration _____

Sales goals _____

Sales orders _____

Relations

Client _____

Customer _____

Employee _____

Labor _____

Vendor _____

Working _____

Time

Delivery time _____

Down time _____

Production time _____

Response time _____

Turnaround time _____

Up time _____

Miscellaneous

Appearance _____

Award _____

Awareness _____

Communications _____

Company image _____

Decision making capability _____

Manufacturing/Production _____

Morale/Motivation _____

Rating _____

Return on assets _____

Return on investment _____

B—Decreased, Eliminated, Reduced, Saved, Protected, Resolved . . .

Cost/Expenditures

Administrative _____

Assembly _____

Capital equipment _____

Compensation _____

Delivery _____

Development _____

Energy _____

Environmental _____

Freight _____

Installation _____

Labor _____

Material _____

Cost/Expenditures

Operating _____

Overhead _____

Sales/Marketing _____

Service _____

Staffing/Recruiting _____

Tooling _____

Warranty _____

Material assets

Inventory _____

Overages _____

Rejects _____

Scrap/Waste _____

Shortages _____

Time

Changeover time _____

Down time _____

Installation time _____

Lost time _____

Overtime _____

Production time _____

Response time _____

Sick time _____

Miscellaneous

Accounts receivable _____

Back orders _____

Bottlenecks _____

Clerical errors _____

Complaints _____

Confidentiality _____

Conflict _____

Credibility _____

Discrepancies _____

Grievances _____

Market share _____

Paperwork _____

Pressure/Tension _____

Profits _____

Recurring problems _____

Reputation/Integrity _____

C—Established, Developed, Implemented, Instructed, Introduced, Revised, Restructured, Restored . . .

Group functions

Circles _____

Classes _____

Departments _____

Facilities _____

Functions _____

Markets _____

Meetings _____

Operations _____

Presentations _____

Programs _____

Seminars _____

Workshops _____

Measurement

Analyses _____

Appraisals _____

Measurement _____

Models _____

Performance _____

Standards _____

Studies _____

Plans/Concepts

Projects _____

Promotions _____

Seminars _____

Strategies _____

Systems _____

Workshops _____

Pricing

Pricing _____

Rates

Rates _____

Printed materials

Agreements _____

Brochures _____

Catalogs _____

Contracts _____

Guidelines _____

Manuals _____

Proposals _____

Publications _____

Reports _____

Reviews _____

Specifications _____

Software

Software _____

Procedures

Applications _____

Backlogs _____

Methods _____

Policies _____

Practices _____

Procedures _____

Processes _____

Studies _____

Systems _____

Techniques _____

Work flow _____

Products/Services

Devices _____

Equipment _____

Machinery _____

Products _____

Services _____

Stating dollars, numbers, and percentages always acts to validate and quantify your statements. If you can figure out a way to include these, by all means do so. This is especially true if you are in a field or area within which numbers are commonly used.

This Accomplishments section is the one to refer to when writing your SOAR statements found in the following and final section of this chapter.

Get Ready to SOAR

Get ready to make your job search take flight!

Wouldn't you like to be able to soar above the competition? It's not all that hard to do, really. If you have completed all of the prior inventory exercises you have already started to taxi down the runway.

The way to beat out your competitors is to *outsell* them. It cannot be stressed often enough and will continue to be stressed—the way to outsell your competition is to be as specific as possible when presenting your sales pitch. Roll out your experiences, skills, personal attributes, and accomplishments and validate each and every one of them. Complete this final exercise and you should be ready and eager to enter the awaiting fray.

SOAR

Americans love acronyms. Here's another one. But, unlike most of the rest, it has the potential to change your life. **SOAR** stands for **S**ubject, **O**verview, **A**ction, and **R**esult. This is the formula to remember and follow throughout your job search. Take an accomplishment, skill, experience, or personal attribute and turn it into a SOAR statement.

For example, as a department head, you proposed and implemented a new bookkeeping procedure resulting in the elimination of one clerical position. That's your accomplishment.

Now, let's suppose an interviewer asks you to cite an accomplishment. Following the SOAR formula, and using the accomplishment cited above, you might (without saying Subject, Overview, Action, and Result before each statement) reply:

Subject: *"I have several accomplishments I'm extremely proud of, but let me tell you about a change I made in our bookkeeping department."*

Overview: *"We were wasting too much time preparing repetitive reports. I decided it was time for a change; a change that would save time, manpower, and money."*

Action: *"Here's what I did. First, I interviewed my department personnel to see if they had any suggestions or ideas. Several of them did. I discovered they were just as disgusted with the constant repetition as I was. I studied their ideas and found the reports in question all had three common elements. Then I discovered it was possible to eliminate three out of five daily reports by making them part of the remaining two."*

Result: *"This resulted in the elimination of one redundant employee, saving the company $25,000 a year. Would you like me to go into more detail?"*

Once again,

s—State the Subject—no more than two sentences. Two or three words is even better.

o—Present a brief Overview—three or four sentences is usually sufficient.

A—Tell what Action you took—keep it brief. Seven or eight descriptive sentences is usually enough. Try to make the listener or reader picture you doing whatever it is you're telling him about. He will have to picture you in a setting he is familiar with. In doing so, if what you say captures his interest, he has subconsciously taken the first step in hiring you. This is because he has already "seen" you working with him and his company.

R—Conclude with the Result—be certain to include dollars, numbers, and percentages whenever you can.

Then, conclude your result statement with a question if possible. For example: "Do you have any questions?" or "Does that answer your question?" or "Would you like me to go into a little more detail?"

Why ask a follow-up question? To try to establish a pattern for the ensuing interview; a pattern wherein you and the interviewer establish a dialogue instead of your being interrogated and placed on the defensive. (This subject is covered in greater depth in Chapter 6, "How to Amaze and Delight Interviewers.")

Directions: Select the accomplishments, skills, personal attributes, or work experiences you are proudest of, that you believe will most impress the listener or reader. Write each as a SOAR statement using the forms provided on the next several pages. Keep each statement brief. You should be able to recite it in no more than 30 to 60 seconds. Make it a habit, beginning right now, to follow up each SOAR statement with an appropriate question.

Do at least ten of these statements using the forms provided. Fifteen or twenty would be even better. After you have worked on each statement, condensing and crystallizing it, transfer it to an index card. Take these cards with you wherever you go and practice them. It is imperative you complete and practice your SOAR statements. They constitute the heart and soul of the job search you are about to embark upon. You'll use them in your resume, cover letters, telephone calls, and in your interviews.

Subject: _____

_____

_____

_____

_____

Overview: _____

_____

_____

_____

_____

Action: _____

_____

_____

_____

_____

Result: _____

_____

_____

_____

_____

Subject: _____

_____

_____

_____

_____

Overview: _____

_____

_____

_____

_____

Action: _____

_____

_____

_____

_____

Result: _____

_____

_____

_____

_____

Subject: _____

_____

_____

_____

Overview: _____

_____

_____

_____

Action: _____

_____

_____

_____

_____

Result: _____

_____

_____

_____

_____

_____

Subject: _____

_____

_____

_____

_____

Overview: _____

_____

_____

_____

_____

Action: _____

_____

_____

_____

_____

Result: _____

_____

_____

_____

_____

Subject: _____

_____

_____

_____

_____

Overview: _____

_____

_____

_____

_____

Action: _____

_____

_____

_____

_____

Result: _____

_____

_____

_____

_____

Subject: _____

_____

_____

_____

_____

Overview: _____

_____

_____

_____

_____

Action: _____

_____

_____

_____

_____

Result: _____

_____

_____

_____

_____

Subject: _____

_____

_____

_____

_____

Overview: _____

_____

_____

_____

_____

Action: _____

_____

_____

_____

_____

Result: _____

_____

_____

_____

_____

Subject: _____

_____

_____

_____

_____

Overview: _____

_____

_____

_____

_____

Action: _____

_____

_____

_____

_____

Result: _____

_____

_____

_____

_____

Subject: _____

_____

_____

_____

_____

Overview: _____

_____

_____

_____

_____

Action: _____

_____

_____

_____

_____

Result: _____

_____

_____

_____

_____

Subject: _____

_____

_____

_____

_____

Overview: _____

_____

_____

_____

_____

Action: _____

_____

_____

_____

_____

Result: _____

_____

_____

_____

_____

Summary

All too often, job seekers try to close the barn door after they've let the horse get away. That is to say, they gradually discover all sorts of good things to say about themselves as their search progresses. This is fine and good, but what about all of the opportunities they may have missed because they didn't have this great information right at the beginning? Who knows whether or not they missed the job of their dreams.

There is absolutely nothing more important to a successful job search than the information solicited in this chapter. You are not going to be hired because you "did a great job." You will not be hired because of what your references have to say about you. They won't even be contacted unless you give employers some reason to contact them. Can you help the company make more money? How? How soon? Prove it. That's the bottom line. Will you be the type of person the boss can get along with? Will you be a fit? How can they be sure? Because of what you have to say about yourself? Talk is cheap. Prove it.

Completing this chapter will take a lot longer than you might like. Don't give up. Stick with it. Do it one section at a time if you must, but above all, do it! This up-front investment of time can get you employed for a much longer time and with far better monetary rewards.

Chapter 2

How to Write an Award-Winning Resume

If you have not completed an intensive self-inventory—your experience, skills, education, and personal characteristics (see Chapter 1), drop everything and do so immediately! If you *have* done this, you should have a list of specific, quantified, validated accomplishments, and **SOAR** statements (written in the following sequence: Subject, Overview, Action, Result). This information will make writing a resume a much easier task.

The Right Way to Use Your Resume

Before you can write a great resume, you must know exactly how you will use it. If you think all you have to do is stick it in a stamped envelope and mail it off to personnel—forget it! The only time you will ever resort to this feeble course of action is when you have absolutely no other available recourse.

Personnel offices are deluged with resumes. Each day brings a new truckload. What chance does your resume have of being the one to elicit positive action? Even if it is terrific, your chances of anything happening are slight, very slight, at best. You will be lucky if a company sends you a form letter thanking you for applying. So, just remember: *No matter how great your resume is, it probably won't do you much good unless it gets directly into the right hands!*

Unless you are looking for a position in human resources or personnel, stay away from this function if at all possible. Keep this thought uppermost in your mind: personnel screens, management hires. This is true for the great majority of companies—especially at the salaried level.

Whenever you can, you must attempt to *hand-carry your resume to the person who will make the hiring decision.* This is the advice given by job search experts to all levels of job seekers. These same experts may not always agree on what makes a perfect resume, but we do agree that hand-carrying your resume to the prospective boss or supervisor is the way to go. Make every effort to arrange a face-to-face meeting. Regrettably, you will usually have to resort to mailing your resume to the decision maker. But first, make every effort to arrange a face-to-face meeting.

Why are experienced job search counselors so adamant on this point? It is all based on the substantiated premise that the head of a particular department or area is the one who actually decides his or her departmental needs and does the hiring for his area. This is so in nearly all cases at just about every company. If you have any work experience at all, you know this to be true.

How do you go about finding out who this person might be? Try networking, using directories, or calling the company and saying, "I'm updating my mailing list. Who is in charge of _____?" (See Chapter 5, "How to Dial Your Way to a Great New Job.")

The Resume as a Road Map

Whenever humanly possible, get the interview *and then* present your resume to the interviewer immediately upon meeting him or her. Because you have skillfully constructed your resume, it will serve as a road map for the interviewer to follow. Because you drew the map and because the interviewer is reading it for the first time, the interview has a much better chance of going in the direction you would like it to go.

Reach Out and Grab Someone

Research indicates that an employer will generally spend no more than ten to twenty seconds glancing at a resume received in the mail. And it might not even be read at all. On those occasions when you must mail your resume, it must gain favorable attention immediately or risk consignment to the reject basket. Therefore, it is mandatory that your resume cry out, "Read Me! Read Me! Read Me!"

To command immediate attention your resume must have visual impact. In retailing, the expression is, "Eye Appeal Is Buy Appeal." Your resume must invite itself to be read. Adherence to the following guidelines will help to achieve this mandatory visual impression.

You Have to Have a Target

The unfortunate truth is, if you do not have a rather definite job target it is virtually impossible to decide what you should be trying to sell. You don't know what the prospective employer is interested in buying. It's like going fishing. If you don't care what kind or how many fish you catch, you can always grab a pole and a can of worms and head for the nearest puddle. But if it's tuna that you desire, you had best get rigged up right, get the right bait, and head out to sea.

Job Objectives—Yes or No

An objective is a target statement that precedes the body of information presented on a resume. For example:

Objective: An entry level accounting position with a major accounting firm.

The danger with making a declaration such as this, is that it can oftentimes hamper your job hunting efforts. What happens, for instance, if you are turned down by all of the major accounting firms? Will some other firm be willing to settle for being your ninth, tenth, or eleventh choice? Will they even consider you? Of course, you could print another resume featuring a new objective—one that eliminates any mention of the major firms.

What if you water down your objective a little? Still bad. A generally vague objective such as the following consumes prime space and priceless time.

> Objective: A challenging management position utilizing effective inter-
> personal and managerial skills and experience leading to
> upward mobility.

What busy employer has the time or the patience to wade through this verbal nonsense? Yet, many resume "experts" insist upon the use of such mealy-mouthed objectives!

Consider this: the objective appears at the top of the paper, right under your contact information, occupying prime real estate. If your resume were a newspaper, merchants would willingly pay dearly for the chance to replace the day's headline with their advertisement.

Should You Use an Objective?

Here are a few guidelines. You decide. You should probably use an objective:

- If you are seeking an entry level position—like a recent college graduate.
- If you are seeking a position not spelled out by the first job title on your resume. For example: If you have been a Sales Representative and would like to move up to a Sales Manager's position you could state:

> Objective: Sales Manager

Other than in these situations, I have difficulty endorsing the use of objectives. Objectives too often make weak, generalized statements such as "a challenging position," "a position utilizing my people skills," or "a position leading to personal and professional growth and advancement." Get to the point! Stop wasting valuable resume space and reading time. If you can't write a specific, targeted objective, don't bother to include one.

Consider this: you can always include an objective statement in the cover letter you write to accompany your resume. The inclusion of an objective in a targeted cover letter not only provides focus, but it also gives you something to say when you could be struggling with finding something to say.

Summaries and Background Statements— Yes or No?

Oftentimes you will find some type of career summary or background statement leading into the body of a resume. For example:

CAREER SUMMARY

Over fifteen years automotive and retail supervisory experience. Skilled administrator possessing excellent verbal and written communication skills. Often complimented for attention to detail and follow-through. Looking for a challenging and rewarding position of responsibility within a fast-track manufacturing environment.

I'm sure you can see that this example is not unlike the objective stated on the prior page. Generally, for the very same reason it is a bad idea to use an objective, it is not a good idea to use a career summary. A career summary similar to this does nothing to make the reader want to continue to read the resume. It often does just the opposite. Resume readers take from ten to twenty seconds to scan a resume. Who could possibly get excited by such a lackluster introduction?

Now, having said that, let's take a look at an *appropriate* use of a career summary or background statement.

CAREER SUMMARY

More than 20 years in progressive materials management. Experienced with United States, European, South American, Pacific Rim, and Japanese vendors. APICS certified. College level instructor in MRP.

What makes this summary acceptable and the one cited before it unacceptable? Although it has a rather generalized introductory sentence, it goes immediately into what looks like a wealth of experience with vendors on an international level. Anyone engaged in manufacturing, especially automotive manufacturing, would recognize that the continents/countries cited are *the* global players of note.

It uses current buzz words or phrases . . . "APICS," "MRP." There's nothing like being on the cutting edge of your industry to catch and maintain an employer's attention. Sometimes a career summary is a good way to immediately tell the reader that you are "with it," or that you have extensive experience in the area in which you hope to land.

In most instances, you will most likely be better off not to include a career or summary statement on your resume. That is my opinion. However, I feel obligated to let you know there are numerous job search consultants who really like to use career summary or background statements.

So, unless you have some very impressive experience directly related to the position you are seeking, you are probably better off not to include a background summary.

Resume Types

For the sake of simplicity, we will group all resumes into three basic types or formats, *standard* (or *chronological*), *prioritized*, and *functional*. Practically every resume follows, or is a variation on, one of these themes.

The Standard (Chronological) Resume

The standard or chronological format is the resume format of choice. It is the format that resume readers like the best. It is sequential in nature—leading from the present or latest position into past positions—each position following the position or company before it according to dates. Because the dates follow one another in downward order it is easy for the reader to note any missing or suspicious dates or periods of employment.

For people who fit the above description, who are moving along a progressive career path, whose next position would be a direct, logical offspring of the most recent position, the standard resume is the type to write.

What if you have a gap in your employment record? This raises a red flag. Why, the reader wonders, is that date missing? Then, the reader immediately rejects you or begins to delve deeply into the resume looking for other suspicious and often disqualifying disparities. And so, if you have some gaps in your job history, it is very easy to be eliminated from consideration when you use the standard format.

The sample resume found on the next page is a standard (more commonly called a chronological) resume. You will notice the dates flow from the present to the past in an uninterrupted manner. Actually, it is a *reverse* chronological resume.)

Standard Resume

DARLENE D. BIRD

5251 Brandeis Road   Hollyfield Hills, CT 88507   (915) 851-1956

FEDERAL–UNITED CORPORATION, Westfield, CT

Administrator, Investor Relations   **1992–Present**
Liaison between transfer agent (bank) and shareholders. Developed programs to increase public awareness of company. Heavily involved with National Investor Relations Institute (NIRI) and National Association of Investors Corporation (NAIC).

- Developed and presented payroll deduction stock purchase program for hourly employees resulting in 50 percent plant enrollment.
- Designed fact brochure for customer/shareholder distribution.
- Maintained 50/50 mix of individual and institutional investors through company promotion at NAIC Investor Fairs.

Supervisor, Corporate Financial Reporting Systems   **1985–1992**
Managed monthly financial consolidation and reporting for Fortune 500 multinational automotive manufacturer/distributor. Coordinated data collection and financial reports. Disseminated information between corporate and manufacturing groups.

Conducted domestic/international software training classes. Selected to implement and debug computerized financial reporting system resulting in:

- $1,000,000 annual reduction in mainframe charges.
- Elimination of 300+ overtime hours and one exempt position.
- Implementation of telecommunication system resulting in 50 percent reduction of telex charges.

Accountant/Coordinator, International Financial Reporting   **1980–1985**
Responsible for monthly financial consolidation and reporting needs. Extensive foreign travel to implement and train personnel on financial reporting software, Micro Control and Quik-Comm.

- Promoted from Accounting Clerk. Administered domestic/foreign ledgers, dividends, royalties, intercompany accounts/billing, accounts receivable/payable, inventory accounting and Canadian accounting, and accounts payable.

EDUCATION

B.A. General Studies—Taxon University, Colchester, FL—1991. Minors: Business Administration and Latin American Studies. Third-year level fluency in Spanish.

If the job you're looking for is the same as, or a logical step up from, the job you last held; and/or if you have a smooth career track record, you should undoubtedly use the standard format.

The Prioritized Resume

The prioritized resume presents the positions held in the order that best represents the job seeker. If you wish to return to a position you held before the most recent one, this is the resume format you should most likely consider.

For example, your present or last position was engineering manager. You hadn't held the position for more than a week when you began to admit to yourself that you hated it. You now long for the "good old days" when all you had to do was engineer and not resolve people problems. Here is an opportunity to return to that position. Your resume choice? Definitely the prioritized. The first position listed on your resume will be that of Engineer. The position following that will probably be your Engineering Manager position. It might even be another position you held before becoming a manager.

If you have worked for the same employer for a lengthy period of time, it's easy to move the positions around. Simply place the company name, city, and your all-inclusive employment dates directly above or directly below your body of information. (See sample on next page.)

Look at the sample prioritized resume once more and note how the same job seeker rearranged her information to place the position she *really* would like to land first. Once again, notice also there are *no* dates after the job titles, just all-inclusive employment dates given after the company name. Using the prioritized format, it is virtually impossible to tell when she held each job.

The stronger your accomplishments, duties, and responsibilities are, the better your chances of having a prioritized resume (or, for that matter, any kind of resume) read. No resume can make a favorable impression if it doesn't have many good things to say about the writer. However, in the case of any resume format other than the standard one, it is doubly essential that what you have to sell outweighs the fact that the dates are missing or don't agree.

Remember, most resume readers frown upon anything other than the standard resume format. But, if you shoot yourself in the foot using it, it won't do you any good. You could be better served by a prioritized resume. Make your decision only after careful deliberation.

Prioritized Resume

DARLENE D. BIRD

5251 Brandeis Road   Hollyfield Hills, CT 88507   (915) 851-1956

FEDERAL–UNITED CORPORATION, Westfield, CT   1980–Present
Supervisor, Corporate Financial Reporting Systems
Managed monthly financial consolidation and reporting for Fortune 500 multi-national automotive manufacturer/distributor. Coordinated data collection and financial reports. Disseminated information between corporate and manufacturing groups.

Conducted domestic/international software training classes. Selected to implement and debug computerized financial reporting system resulting in:

- $1,000,000 annual reduction in mainframe charges. Elimination of 300+ overtime hours and one exempt position.
- Implementation of telecommunication system resulting in 50 percent reduction of telex charges.

Administrator, Investor Relations
Liaison between transfer agent (bank) and shareholders. Developed programs to increase public awareness of company. Heavily involved with National Investor Relations Institute (NIRI) and National Association of Investors Corporation (NAIC).

- Developed and presented payroll deduction stock purchase program for hourly employees resulting in 50 percent plant enrollment.
- Designed fact brochure for customer/shareholder distribution.
- Maintained 50/50 mix of individual and institutional investors through company promotion at NAIC Investor Fairs.

Accountant/Coordinator, International Financial Reporting
Responsible for monthly financial consolidation and reporting needs. Extensive foreign travel to implement and train personnel on financial reporting software, Micro Control and Quik-Comm.

- Promoted from Accounting Clerk. Administered domestic/foreign ledgers, dividends, intercompany accounts/billing, accounts receivable/payable, inventory accounting and Canadian accounting, and accounts payable.

EDUCATION/SEMINARS

BA—General Studies—Taxon University, Colchester, FL—1991. Minors: Business Administration and Latin American Studies. Third-year level fluency in Spanish.

Administrator training: 3–Com, Novell, IBM Token–Ring Networks. Experienced in: Lotus 1–2–3, Harvard Graphics, and WordPerfect.

The Functional Resume

If you have performed the same types of duties and responsibilities in several jobs, or are trying to land a position unlike those you have held, consider using a functional resume.

For example, suppose several of your positions required that you do many of the same types of things. Secretaries are a good example of this. Typing, word processing, filing, answering the phone, handling travel arrangements and accommodations are the types of activities many secretarial positions require. To keep repeating these activities in a resume makes for pretty dull reading.

In a functional resume, you can place similar activities under specific categories, *no matter when or where these experiences were obtained.* Group the activities into categories such as: Training, Secretarial, Data Processing, Scheduling, etc. A functional resume can alleviate boring reading and arouse reader interest.

When writing a functional resume, place the function most directly related to the position you are seeking at the top of the page. In other words, if you have both data processing and supervisory experience and are looking for a supervisory position, you would lead off with this category. This is the same approach used when writing a prioritized resume. Study the example found on the next page.

Whichever resume format you use, it is only as effective as what you have to sell to the reader. Of course, "eye" appeal is "buy" appeal. Make your document as attractive and appealing as possible, but once you have captured the employer's attention, you had better be ready to sell.

Other Resume Considerations

Introductory Information

The first block of information on your resume—after your name, address, and telephone number(s)—should contain data that most directly relates to the position you are seeking. Once in a while it will be an objective or a career summary. But, for most job seekers, it will be the title of the job they have just left or a closely related position.

New and recent college graduates will use their college education in this lead-off spot—if it pertains to the position they are

Functional Resume

MICHAEL C. COUGHLAN

7387 Edinborough
West Bloomburg, PA 32322

Home: (313) 855-2842
Office: (313) 362-2187

General Manager
Total operational responsibility for two $2MM Plastic Blow-Molding manufacturing facilities, including Manufacturing, Prototype, Quality, and Engineering.
- Full P&L responsibility.
- Automotive OEM Supplier to Ford & Chrysler.
- Ford Q–1 rating maintained.

General Manager
Responsible for total operations of $8MM wire products division including Manufacuring, Marketing, Engineering, and Finance.
- Full P&L responsibility.
- Division established Sales/Earnings/ROI records.

Controller
Responsible for all accounting functions of $18MM Sheet Metal Stamping Manufacturer and Automotive OEM Supplier.
- Prepared long-range business plan for TFE survey.

Division Controller
Division included refrigeration plant ($100MM in sales and 1,100 employees) and 5 outlying plants and 18 sales branches.
- Developed company-wide "Yes We Can" cost reduction program to improve margins and operating income.
- Coordinated preparation of annual profit plans for all locations, including review and final approval by top management.

Accounting Manager
Responsible for all accounting functions of $100MM, 1.5MM square foot plant, 1,100 employees.

Accounting Supervisor
Responsible for all General Accounting Department functions, including liaison between Corporate Headquarters and outside auditors.

Employment History

KENT PLASTICS, Coronet, PA	1995–98
BARKLEY TUBING, Coronet, PA	1990–95
HUNTINGTON CORPORATION, Bridgeport, PA	1985–90
LARKIN & STEARNS, CPAs, Dublin, OH	1981–85
PRICE WATERHOME, CPAs, Columbus, OH	1978–81

Education
MSC: Finance—St. Paul University – St. Paul, MN
BA: Accounting—Benton College—Benton, AR
CPA: University of Arkansas
Dale Carnegie: Human Relations/Management Courses. Graduate Assistant.

seeking. Unlike most experienced job seekers, they should also consider placing an objective in the beginning. After all, with little or no work experience, it is difficult for the reader to ascertain what type of job they are looking for if they don't give an objective.

Once again, bear in mind that the opening introductory statement on your resume must contain information to immediately grab the reader's attention. Tell what you want; don't play games. Don't force the reader to resort to ESP to discover what position you are seeking.

Placement and job search counselors sometimes lose sight of the fact that a resume is intended to act on the job seeker's behalf, not the employer's. It should contain only information that can win you an interview. It should not contain information that makes it easy for the reader to screen you out. Your goal is to make the reader eager to meet and find out more about you.

Dates

Unless you changed jobs several times in the middle of the year(s) there is really no need to include the months when you began and ended each job. Years will suffice.

If you are on severance you are technically still on the company payroll. So, after the beginning date of your most recent job, print the word "Present." For example:

CONTROLLER   1995–Present

Companies frequently give hiring preference to job seekers who are currently employed, although, given the job market in the last decade, they have become more accustomed to hiring unemployed people.

If you are out of work and no longer on the company payroll, you should cite the year you left the company:

CONTROLLER   1995–97

If you have done a lot of job-hopping or have gaps in your employment record you should consider trying to write a resume that minimizes or eliminates dates. Just realize that employers prefer the standard or chronological resume. They have neither the time nor the inclination to try to read between the lines.

Action Words

The inclusion of appropriate action words or SOAR statements, which you should have compiled prior to beginning your resume, will give life to your presentation. Don't use the same statements or action words over and over again . . . supervised this . . . supervised that, and so on. Use expressions such as "supervised," "directed," and "managed."

Company Names

My preference is to set company names in capital letters followed by the city and dates in upper and lower case:

BRAXTON MANUFACTURING, INC., Elysia, IL 1995–Present

You may place the company names before, beside, or after each job title. It is up to you to decide what serves your purpose and what you think looks the best. A glance at the sample resumes offered at the end of this chapter will give you an idea of how others have handled this topic.

Job Titles

I like job titles all caps, bold-faced, and underlined. I know, underlining typesetting is a "no-no," but we're not talking about pleasing your college English professor. We're talking about getting somebody to read your resume. Your future depends on it. So, forget about the rules, except for punctuation and grammar. I happen to like the way that judicious underlining makes job titles stand out.

Let's create a job title format that will invite itself to be read. Here's how a title would look both ways, underlined and not underlined. Take your pick. Choose the style you like best.

<u>CHIEF COOK/BOTTLE WASHER</u>   1989–95

or

CHIEF COOK/BOTTLE WASHER   1989–95

Duties and Responsibilities

Think back upon what you did each day on your former or present job(s). What actions did you take? What tools or instruments were involved? Who did you work for or with? What were the results?

If you performed above and beyond what was expected of you, turn these actions into accomplishments.

Accomplishments

When you have accomplishments to sell, sell them: *increased, eliminated, saved, reduced, exceeded.* Use SOAR statements—Subject, Overview, Action, Result. Bullet them to make them stand out. Indent the bulleted statements from both the left and right margins to frame them with a little white space to draw the reader's eye right to them. You may even wish to place "Accomplishments" in bold letters preceding them. Use dollars, numbers, and percentages. Show how you can add to the bottom line. *There is nothing more important to a resume than specific accomplishments that show specific results.*

Education

Education beyond the high school level should be stated. If you did not graduate but completed a few years or courses, simply state the name of the program you were enrolled in, the name of the institution, and the city and state it is in. If your education is ancient history, you might be wise to simply leave out the date(s) when you graduated.

If you participated in career-advancing seminars or workshops, these should also be listed by name, who taught them (if significant), and if of recent vintage, the dates (years only) when you participated. Unless these courses were lengthy, don't include the number of days that they were held. Include both in-house and off-site classes.

Honors and Awards

Be sure to include any special honors and/or awards you have received relative to your employment. State the name of the award and the date received. Remember to include any special employee task force or team you were assigned to or for which you volunteered.

Publications and Patents

You may have authored some articles or reports pertinent to your job objective. Perhaps you were responsible for obtaining a patent or patents. If you have enough of these items you might want to consider adding an addendum to your resume. If you haven't enough to make this addendum impressive, you can always include all of your education followed by your publications or patents.

Affiliations

Do you belong to a professional association? A fraternal or civic organization? Unless it is religiously oriented, you should include it. Be certain to include any offices you might have held or any special committees you chaired or served on.

Volunteer Work

Even if this experience does not relate to your job target, it still presents you in a favorable light. Like work experience, start with your most recent volunteer experience and go back in time—unless an earlier experience is more directly applicable.

Include: volunteer/job title (if any)—organization name—dates of volunteer work—organization description—volunteer work description—duties and responsibilities (these may be included under volunteer work description)—accomplishments and achievements—special commendations.

Military History

Only include if you were honorably discharged. Specify: branch of service—dates of service—assignments and locations—rank(s)—duties and responsibilities—military schooling.

Hobbies and Interests

Add if applicable to position sought, if you need filler material, or if you believe it will stimulate conversation. (Did you know that George M. Cohan gave preference to male actors for his shows based upon whether they could contribute on the field to his baseball team?)

References and Salary Requirements

Entry level job seekers may wish to include references when mailing a resume. All other job seekers—don't bother. You will be asked for references once the employer is interested in hiring you.

When requesting references, employers want first and foremost to see your business or work references. But, because of fear of what they say being held against them in court, most employers simply refuse to release such information. Save your references for during or after the interview. They could help to build a stronger on-site case for being hired.

Never present salary requirements in a cover letter, a resume, or when responding to a help-wanted ad. It's too easy to eliminate yourself from contention by stating an amount that's too high or too low.

Layout or Appearance

There is no definite, absolute format that dictates how you have to write your resume or what it should look like. You can choose any approach you like. Select a format that best represents your interests. If you attempt to get clever or extremely original, most employers will immediately reject your offering.

An exception to straightforward resumes might be made for those job seekers in the fields of advertising, show business, or public relations. Here, creative thinking is a welcomed commodity and daring to be different can be appreciated.

Finally, leave plenty of white space; let it breathe. Keep it short—one page if at all possible. Never more than two. Have it typeset or print it on a letter quality or laser printer. Don't use more than two type styles, and don't use huge letters, exotic borders, or excessive underlining.

Techniques for Keeping a Resume Short

1. *Eliminate the "I's" and "my's."* "I reported to the Director of Finance" becomes simply, "Reported to the Director of Finance." Also eliminate as many "and's" and "the's" as possible.
2. *Use occasional slashes (/).* In reviewing the sample resumes you will note how two or more duties, functions, or activi-

ties can be placed next to each other with a "/" instead of a conjunction such as "the" between them. Thus, "Conducted domestic and international software classes" becomes, "Conducted domestic/international software classes."

3. ***Hyphenate an occasional word or two.*** Never allow more than two consecutive sentences to end in hyphens. Never have more than three or four hyphens per page. I told you to avoid using "the," "of," "both," etc., because they slow down reading. Now I'm telling you it may actually be desirable to insert a "the," "of," "both," and so on to avoid excessive hyphenation.

When you justify the right margin the computer will stretch words and spaces throughout the line so that each line manages to end at the right, directly under the line above it. In doing so, the line often winds up with wider than acceptable gaps or white spaces between words. This is unsightly and, worse yet, slows down the reading. Use a ragged right margin. But this also can be a problem because, once in a while, a line or two will "stick out" farther than the other lines.

There are two basic ways to try to have a right margin as close to justified as possible:

- Rewrite the offending sentence leaving out, inserting, or changing words but not changing its meaning.
- Change the margins. However, don't end up with skinny left and right margins that allow you to place too much ink on the page, destroying your document's appearance.

Now you should see how it's possible to pack a lot more on one page than one might suspect—still leaving ample white space so that you don't drown the reader in a sea of ink—and without using small type or cramming things together. *Avoid small type sizes at all costs.* If the type is too small, it won't be read. Use 12 point or perhaps 10 point type, but don't go any smaller. Also avoid fancy, hard-to-read fonts, like italics or script.

Resume Guidelines

Brevity—one page if possible. Never more than two.

Clean type—laser or letter quality printer, electric typewriter, or typeset. No smudges or erasures.

Quality reproduction—done on the printer's best copy machine, or printed "fresh" for every application.

Quality stationery—resume, cover letter, and envelope all of the same quality stock of a subdued color.

Spelling—perfect.

Punctuation—perfect.

Grammar—correct.

Key titles and names—all caps, bold-faced, underlined if you like them that way.

Bullets—preceding especially important information such as specific accomplishments. Do not create a page of wall-to-wall bullets. Overuse defeats their purpose—to draw attention to some very specific point or points.

White space—ample margins and internal white space. Don't drown the reader in a sea of ink.

Dates/numbers/percentages—break up the monotony imposed by words, words, and more words—especially if you have a numbers type background and it is fairly impressive. Be certain to quantify as many of your duties, responsibilities, and accomplishments as possible.

Minimize articles—eliminate "and," "of," "the," etc., whenever possible.

Personal pronouns—none.

Action words—use words that invoke action imagery: *created, initiated,* and *analyzed.* Or, in the present tense, *creating, initiating,* and *analyzing.*

Summary

Always present your resume, in person, to the person in charge of your area of interest. In doing so, you prevent rejection by mail while providing a road map for the interview.

- If you have to mail your resume, always mail it to the person in charge of your interest area. Be certain to address him or her correctly as Dr., Mr., Mrs., Miss, or Ms.—spell the name correctly—include his or her correct job title.

- Your resume must contain a telephone number, or numbers, where you, or someone delegated to represent you, can be reached during the day.
- The information immediately following the opening block of personal contact information should be composed of data most directly related to your job target.
- Your resume must contain only information that sells.
- Your resume must invite immediate reading. It should cry out, "Read Me! Read Me! Read Me!"
- Your resume should make the reader want to know more about you.

Your resume is your sales piece. Be proud of it!

Sample Resumes

Here are some exemplary resumes for you to review. Note that I said "review," not copy. Pay particular attention to:

- amount of white space
- clarity of the type
- action words
- succinct, action-oriented sentences
- use of bulleted accomplishments, and, sometimes, duties and responsibilities
- use of boldface, uppercase, and underlining
- use of dollars, numbers, and percentages wherever possible and impressive
- brevity of the document

Some of these samples are two pages in length, but only when the content helps to sell the reader. And, when there is a second page, it also must invite itself to be read using all of the above techniques. Don't use a two-page format unless absolutely necessary. Usually, the higher up the corporate ladder you are, the more likely you can justify writing a two-pager. But, if you can tell your story and sell it on one page, do it.

Verice (Prioritized/Functional, page 72)

She thinks her education is the most important thing she has to promote for the type of position she is looking for (stated in her cover letter), so she leads off with this. Then she arranges her job titles in the order most directed to the position she is seeking. It isn't apparent unless you stop to study it, but she has presented positions she held and functions she held interchangeably. For example, "Personnel Supervision" is a function and "Public Relations Director" is a specific position. She presents a list of her employers after she has sold herself and then, once again, in the sequence most related to her job target. It's true, she may turn some readers off because, aside from her education, she has omitted dates. She felt, however, if she did include the dates she would be "shot down" anyway.

Thomas (Standard—version 1, pages 73, 74)

This is a straightforward two-page resume. In her first draft, she attempted to squeeze everything onto one page by eliminating the space between the bulleted achievements, but it looked too crowded. In her two most recent positions she breaks her introductory information into two, and then three, separate paragraphs of only a few sentences each. If she had not done this, the information may have led to a third page, something I believe should be avoided at all cost. Her earliest positions would present some pretty boring ancient history. So, instead, she turns these two insignificant positions into a bulleted statement. Why not? Being promoted is an accomplishment!

Thomas (Standard with Objective—version two, pages 75, 76)

This resume is almost identical to the prior one. However, she makes use of an objective to let the reader know she would be happy to obtain a regular sales position, even though she was a supervisor in her most recent position. She also eliminates a few bulleted accomplishments that she felt would hurt her quest for a sales position by making her appear overqualified. Then, unlike the prior version, she eliminated the space between the bulleted items to conserve space.

David (Standard, pages 77, 78)

He has differentiated between duties/responsibilities and accomplishment statements by placing dashes before the first and bullets before the latter. He further highlights his accomplishments by using an accomplishment heading to introduce them. He feels his most recent position is by far the most pertinent one as he is looking for a similar position. So, he expands upon this position and includes his previous positions in a two-sentence paragraph concluding his opening block of information. By doing so, he has framed the dashed and indented statements with two blocks of margin-to-margin type. Presented this way, his most powerful sales material immediately attracts the reader's attention. It probably wouldn't make too much difference if his second page got lost. But, page two is a no-brainer as far as ease of reading is concerned and shows some impressive awards.

Kennedy (Standard, page 79)

Another straightforward presentation using bulleted statements in the opening, most important material. Being an auditor, he attempted to include numbers whenever he could.

Gomez (Standard/Functional, page 80)

He tells you right away—boldface and uppercase—what he is and what he is looking for. Then, the company name and dates and then, a background summary (although he doesn't title it as such). His experience covers a good number of years and so he decides to break it into functional blocks, each followed by a brief description of what he did, followed by bulleted accomplishments. Look at the left margin. Note how he formatted his page so that the function headings and bulleted accomplishments jump off the page. He was fortunate enough to have some quantifiable accomplishments and, to his credit, he led off with the numbers followed by the descriptions. He also framed his opening accomplishments by indenting them and sandwiching them between two regular paragraphs. The bulleted statements stand out even more because he has severely indented the introductory paragraph leading into them. There's some pretty subtle and effective stuff going on here.

Bright (Standard, page 81)

Traditional approach. One page. Easy-to-read. The reader assumes the writer is looking for a position the same as, or directly related to, her most recent one. Accomplishment oriented, she manages to include a few percentages in her accomplishment statements.

Wisenhauser (Standard, page 82)

One page. Easy-to-read. Results oriented. Capped off with an impressive listing of workshops or seminars attended. This is especially important. Her degree is in a somewhat unrelated area and not of recent vintage. She must strive to look knowledgeable and current in the area she has targeted.

Bird (Prioritized, page 83)

This is the same prioritized resume found earlier in this chapter. I included it here to show you how nice it can look even when it is not typeset. Also, by not typesetting it, it is possible to produce it on one attractive page. I used asterisks instead of bullets here just to let you know that a bullet doesn't have to be a black circle. I once worked on an art graduate's resume that used old-fashioned pen heads, ☞, to bullet his important information.

Bird (Standard, page 84)

A typed version of the same standard resume located earlier in this chapter.

Hollander (Functional, pages 85, 86)

Note the very first word on this resume: *Confidential*. This warns the reader that this individual is still employed by the company he will tell about. He doesn't want the reader to call the company and ask questions about him for fear of losing his job before he finds a new one. He opens the body of the resume with the company name and dates of employment centered at the top of the page. Although all of the names and dates have been changed on these resumes, I can tell you why he made this so prominent. Being employed by one of the nation's best known retailers, he wanted to accent this. His introductory statement is really a background summary without the customary heading.

He bold-faces the foreign countries he has dealt with. This is important information given today's job climate, particularly in the garment industry. Not too many items of clothing are actually produced in the states today. Then he states, in boldface, his areas of expertise, a concluding paragraph, his accomplishments, and a catch-all category that he calls, "Additional Responsibilities." His second page is extremely easy to read and is little more than a listing of positions he has held.

Strom (Standard, page 87)

This resume illustrates how someone with as many duties and responsibilities as a Plant Manager can still write a powerful one-page resume. It also illustrates the effective use of numbers. The word for this resume is "tight."

Bailey (Standard, page 88)

Here, the resume writer has sandwiched and highlighted his bulleted duties and responsibilities between an opening and a closing paragraph of text. He felt that his prior positions were not all that important so he just listed them. But even with these he tried to attach some significance by concluding each with the word "Promoted," bold-faced. Under education, which is not job related, he has also included more specific, job-related classes. He bold-faced these for added emphasis. Because he had a lot of white space at the bottom of the page, he filled it in by adding, "References Furnished Upon Request."

Cohen (Standard, pages 89, 90)

Another typical standard resume layout. See how each of his accomplishment statements leads off with an action word and how no two action words are alike. Page two is really easy on the eyes and would not scare many resume readers away—especially because he has made such an impressive case for himself on the first page. This writer's military background is most impressive and will surely lead to some interesting ice-breaking dialogue with interviewers.

Lenhardt (Standard, page 91)

One page. Inviting to be read. Accomplishments bulleted. Company names and job titles bold-faced and uppercase. Also, note how the body of text under each is indented just a little so that the titles stand out. Then, the accomplishments are indented yet again. He believes that the jobs he held before the last two would not impress an employer so he doesn't belabor what he did in these positions.

Lewis (Prioritized, pages 92, 93)

This two-pager, with the positions centered and highlighted and the companies centered under them, contains some powerful sales material. However, if you look closely, you will see there are no dates given for any of the employment history. Why? The job he is looking for is the same as an earlier job and not the last one he held. Fearing that the employer would be turned off by this, he elected to take a chance, prioritize his positions, and hope what he has to sell will outweigh the problem of missing dates. The second page contains some good sales material and is easy to read.

Reimerez (Standard, page 94)

Because he has only one year experience following graduation, he places his degree first. Also, the degree is directly related to his job target. Under his degree he cites some of the courses he has taken because they are directly related to his target. Although he had only a year of actual work experience, he certainly has made the most of it—including dressing it up with a few numbers here and there. The bulleted statements are framed by the opening and closing paragraphs of text. The reader should also be impressed by this young candidate's membership background.

Jackson (Prioritized/Functional, page 95)

This job seeker had held the same position for too many years. In fact, he had very little experience in his field other than performing the same type of activities over and over. He felt it necessary to use an objective and to categorize his basic areas of experience. Under each, he inserted some background information no matter when he had it or how many times he did it. The situation presented under "Layout/Methods" was his sole moment in the spotlight, so it is given as much real estate as possible. There was certainly no justification for this resume writer to go over onto a second page. If you haven't already noticed, see how the experience section of the resume is indented even more than the headings. This allowed him to avoid "padding" to make a good impression.

Kahn (Functional, page 96)

I call this a functional format, but it actually is a hybrid. She really goes out on a limb, leading off with a heading she calls "Representative Professional Accomplishments." Taking what she hopes will be impressive information from her background, no matter where or when she obtained it, she presents it here, bulleting it and separating each of the four statements. She follows up with minimal information about places of employment stating just her job titles. This resume is short and easy to read, but will it turn the reader on or off? Obviously, some extenuating circumstance(s) led her to take a gamble on this very unusual format.

Brown (Functional, page 97)

He immediately states he is looking for a Sales/Marketing Management position. This is followed by his employer's name and all-inclusive dates of employment. When he wrote this resume he was no longer working for the company. However, he was receiving severance pay and thus, was still on the company payroll. Being on the payroll, he feels justified in stating "Present" after the date when he started with the company. He uses a background summary, something I am not too fond of; but this one is brief with some punch to it. Then, he states the positions he held— centered, in uppercase, and bold-faced. What he is saying to the reader is, "If you have a need for someone in any of these positions, I have the experience. I'm the person you're looking for." This opens the window of opportunity much wider for him. Then, he breaks his background into three functional areas, each with an introductory statement followed by bulleted achievements. Finally, he concludes very simply with his degrees, where he obtained them, and when. This is a marketing resume but, by rearranging the job sequence, he could easily use it for engineering or sales.

MARGARET (MARGE) VERICE

1039 Bevanston Road, Apt. 16
Blackston, Michigan 40002
(787) 787-7878

EDUCATION

MA: Human Service Management   (3.8 GPA)   Nazarene College   1995
BS: Psychology & Communication   (3.5 GPA)   Western Michigan   1987

Facility/Program Development Management
Responsible for preparing and implementing $100,000+ budget for both a 216-
and 109-acre campsite. Established goal-oriented programs and property main-
tenance plans according to professional, state, and public health standards.
  • Accomplished a 57% increase in resident camp attendance within a three-
    year period.
  • Developed annual program for physically/mentally impaired campers.

Personnel Supervision
Recruited and supervised 40+ employees. Developed job descriptions, policies,
salary ranges, orientation, training, and incentive and retention programs. Recruited,
trained, and supported board and committee volunteers for specific tasks.

Public Relations Director
Created written copy and design of forms, brochures, newsletters, and annual
reports. Presented mission of organization through networking, public speak-
ing, and press releases.
  • Coordinated product sales and fund development campaigns.
  • Produced highly successful slide show and promotional packages.

Milieu (Recreation/Education) Therapist
Developed objectives and conducted recreational, educational, and social pro-
grams. Performed ongoing assessments to develop an environment conducive
to the restoration of mental health.
  • Established volunteer program.
  • Developed internship program in cooperation with universities.
  • Prepared and submitted proposals and grant applications.

Employers: BLACKSTON REHABILITATION CENTER, Blackston, MI
              MICHIGAN PROGRAM FOR TEENS, Cooper, MI
              GIRL SCOUTS OF AMERICA, Blackston, MI

ASSOCIATIONS

Calverton Alcohol and Drug Abuse Council: Board Member
Michigan Association of Active Professionals
National Association of Therapeutic Counselors
Association of Girl Scouts: Executive Staff

KARLA A. THOMAS

570 Prospect Avenue
Milwaukee, Wisconsin 59002
(418) 125-3473

AMERICAN PUBLISHING, INC., Gladden, WI   **1995–Present**

Account Supervisor—Regional Sales Group
Division of American Corporation, Chicago, IL. Regional Sales Group selling directory listings to 400 automotive related manufacturers in four states. Annual billings in excess of $23 million.

Prospect, promote, and sell classified and display directory advertising in Wisconsin. Manage existing client base of more than 55 national and regional advertisers. Report to Vice President Sales—Eldorado, NM.

Interact with prospects, clients, and advertising agencies. Develop and present strategic proposals including sales, marketing, communications, and directory objectives.

- Achieved 20% increase in 1994 billings realizing $500,000 in sales.
- Increased profits an average of 5–10% per account, by reducing discounts.
- Reestablished sales presence in Wisconsin with premise contacts for existing and prospective accounts.
- Reduced 60+ day receivables to .008 of account base.

BBRC CORPORATION, Des Plaines, IL   **1994–95**

Regional Sales Specialist—BBRC Compugraphic Division
A Thompson-Sayers, USA Company marketing electronic pre-press equipment worldwide: high resolution laser imagesetters, scanners, expansion boards, hardware/software, and peripheral products serving users in the graphics industry.

Directed Midwest telemarketing program to prospect, promote, and sell computer typesetting and graphic imaging systems. Assisted two field sales representatives in generating incremental territory sales.

- Awarded Blue Ribbon as one of top performers in country during 1st quarter, 1995.
- Ranked #3 in Central Region during 1st quarter, 1995.

COLBY ADVERTISING, Brimfield, WI   **1988–94**

Director—Brand Marketing Division
Supervised account team of 10 responsible for division's annual billings of $10M. Conceptualized National Brand programs. Active in new business development and presentations.

- Secured $2M in new business in 4th quarter of 1990.
- Instrumental in division's growth via existing and new clients.

Manager
Supervised and trained Account Executives and Marketing Interns. Delivered key account presentations with client's sales and marketing teams. Responsible for retail specific program development and implementation.

- Project leader for $5M program with five Account Executives as direct reportees.
- Project led to Canadian expansion—equivalent to a $6M national U.S. program.
- Promoted from Senior Account Executive and Account Executive.

Clients included Gordon Personal Care Division, Black & White Household Products Group, 3K Magnetic Media Division, S&S Fine Foods, 3K Canada Inc.— Consumer Products & Home Entertainment Divisions, Bentley Brands Bread Products Division.

EDUCATION
BBA: Eastern Wisconsin University—Yardley, WI—1988

Marketing Major—Concentration: Sales/Sales Management

PROFESSIONAL AFFILIATIONS
Milwaukee Advertising Club

Board Member: Gladden Reading Alliance

Standard with Objective

KARLA A. THOMAS

570 Prospect Avenue
Milwaukee, Wisconsin 59002
(418) 125-3473

Objective: Sales position providing opportunity for account development and cultivating long-term business partnerships.

AMERICAN PUBLISHING, INC., Gladden, WI   **1995–Present**

Account Supervisor—Regional Sales Group

Division of American Corporation, Chicago, IL. Regional Sales Group selling directory listings to 400 automotive related manufacturers in four states. Annual billings in excess of $23M.

Prospect, promote, and sell classified and display directory advertising in Wisconsin. Manage existing client base of more than 55 national and regional advertisers. Report to Vice President Sales—Eldorado, NM.

Interact with prospects, clients, and advertising agencies. Develop and present strategic proposals including sales, marketing, communications, and Yellow Page directory objectives.

• Achieved 20% increase in 1996 billings realizing $500,000 in sales.

• Increased profits an average of 5–10% per account by reducing discounts.

BBRC CORPORATION, Des Plaines, IL   **1994–95**

Regional Sales Specialist—BBRC Compugraphic Division

A Thompson-Sayers, USA Company marketing electronic pre-press products worldwide: high resolution laser imagesetters, scanners, expansion boards, hardware/software, and peripheral equipment serving users in the graphics industry.

Directed Midwest telemarketing program to prospect, promote, and sell computer typesetting and graphic imaging systems. Assisted two field sales representatives in generating incremental territory sales.

• Awarded Blue Ribbon as one of top performers in country during 1st quarter, 1995.

• Ranked #3 in Central Region, 1st quarter, 1995.

COLBY ADVERTISING, Southfield, MI   **1988–94**

Director—Brand Marketing Division

Supervised account team of 10 responsible for division's annual billings of $10M. Conceptualized National Brand programs. Active in new business development presentations.

• Secured $2M in new business in 4th quarter of 1990.

• Instrumental in division's growth via existing and new clients.

Manager
Supervised and trained Account Executives and Marketing Interns. Delivered key account presentations with client's sales and marketing teams. Responsible for retail specific program development and implementation.

- Project leader for $5M program with five Account Executives as direct reportees. Project led to Canadian Expansion.

Promoted from **Senior Account Executive** and **Account Executive**

Clients included Gordon Personal Care Division, Black & White Household Products Group, 3K Magnetic Media Division, S&S Fine Foods, 3K Canada Inc.— Consumer Products & Home Entertainment Divisions, Bentley Brands Bread Products Division.

EDUCATION
BBA: Eastern Wisconsin University—Marketing Major
Concentration: Sales/Sales Management, 1988

PROFESSIONAL AFFILIATIONS
Milwaukee Advertising Club
Board Member: Gladden Reading Alliance

DARION DAVID

15401 Lincoln, Woodson, IN 48227   (303) 270-4155 or (303) 646-2121

Senior Art Director
J & J ADVERTISING AGENCY   1993–Present

Assigned to 15-member Creative Department handling Woodland Motor Homes, International Division, account. Responsibilities include designing/implementing television, national magazine, catalog, and outdoor advertising. Also responsible for directing art for Woodland Motor Homes'"See America from Your Front Room" program and merchandising. Additional experience includes:

— Coordinating post production TV storyboards and art direction on shooting locations.

— Preparing budgets and cost estimates for production and client presentations.

— Editing film, music, and voice-overs.

— Designing and constructing promotional displays.

Entered agency as Photo Stat Technician. Subsequently promoted to **Art Director** and **Senior Art Director**.

ACCOMPLISHMENTS

• Instrumental in researching and developing mobile homes company promotional campaign resulting in new $4MM annual account.

• Assisted in developing and implementing system for formulating prospective account presentations.

• Investigated and recommended art supply purchases reducing associated costs by 75%.

• Devised new mat art arrangement with 50% annual savings.

Commercial Artist
MAGIC INK ILLUSTRATORS, INC.   1988–93

Studio artist and keyliner. Represented studio as sales representative. Estimated budget and project costs submitting written estimates.

Darion David
page two of two

EDUCATION
Coldbrook Academy of Art. Indian Hills, IN
Film Animation and TV Production Labs

Oakdale Community College. Forest Hills, IN
Art Direction and Photographic Lighting

Adcraft SouthWood Institute. Broyles, IN
Media Advertising Seminar

Oliver Newton College. Brookfield, IN
B.F.A. Advertising Marketing

AWARDS
"Best Teller." Broad View catalog award. 1999.

"Maddy." Retail catalog award. 1997.

"Clio." "Woodland: Fast Track" (:30 sec. TV). 1996.

"Silver Cup." (Print.) 1996.

"Innovative Ad of the Year." 1994.

MEMBERSHIPS/ACTIVITIES
Adcraft Club of Indianapolis

Maddy Club

Indianapolis Council of the Arts

Indianapolis Urban League

ROBERT EDWARD KENNEDY

20000 Five Stars   **Office: (513) 352-2187**
Lowell, MA 01775   **Home: (513) 255-1810**

CONGLOMERATE CORPORATION
1992–Present

Corporate Auditor   **1997–Present**

Plan, organize, and direct domestic operational and financial audits at 26 manufacturing facilities, 43 warehouses, and at corporate level. Train/Supervise audit personnel, reviewing all paperwork. Evaluate internal controls, variance analyses, and cost development. Responsibilities also include:

- Documenting, preparing, and presenting audit recommendations and reports to all levels of management.
- Conducting follow-up audits to ensure compliance with recommendations.
- Analyzing manufacturing floor reporting.
- Working closely with public auditors reducing year-end auditing cost 5 to 20%.

Division Accounting Supervisor   **1995–97**

Planned, coordinated, and reviewed all work activities for three exempt and seven non-exempt employees. Forecasted and prepared $6 Million annual operational budget for division administrative staff. Also responsible for analyzation of earnings for five domestic facilities involving up to $330 Million annual sales. Interacted with division department managers investigating and resolving budget variances and deviations.

Plant Cost Accountant   **1992–95**

Developed "work-center" material, labor, and overhead cost standards. Monitored standards, reporting monthly deviations to appropriate plant management. Worked with Industrial Engineers developing capital expenditure cost justification data. Assisted in control of physical assets movement in and between facilities.

EDUCATION:

MA—Business Management. Central Michigan University. 1994

BBA—Business Administration. Wareham State College. 1992

RICARDO GOMEZ

98989 Irma Road

H: (213) 123-4567   **Fair Haven, NM 98980**   O: (213) 234-4321

CHEMICAL TECHNOLOGIST

FIBERGLASS WORKS, INC. Research Division, Apache, NM   1979–Present
Twenty years' experience in chemical analysis and process support services with state's largest glass insulation products supplier.

Chemical Analysis: Evaluated alternative raw materials and process to ensure future effectiveness, resulting in:

- $1,000,000/yr cost savings in dye consumption.
- $5,000,000/yr cost savings with off-shore resin supply.
- 70% reduction in emulsifier consumption.
- 15–20% increase in productivity with decreased cure time.

Audited incoming raw materials resulting in significant reduction in "off spec" chemicals being supplied to operating plants.

Training/Supervision: Responsible for the organization and supervision of binder process audits for all wool plants. Audits allowed the transfer of new technology to operating personnel, assuring that operations conformed to procedures and formulas. Duties:

- Trained employees in the operation of new systems and technology.
- Calculated/estimated/tailored adhesive systems to aid in product rationalization resulting in $2,000,000/yr cost improvement.
- Evaluated/issued test methods and procedures for plant operations.

Communications: Established liaison between the shift operators and management to implement process improvement teams as a natural follow-up to SPC and TQM.

EDUCATION AND SEMINARS

BS: Lambton College of Applied Arts and Technology
Sarnia, Ontario, Canada

Statistical Process Control.   1992

Hunterlab Color Seminar.   1990

COMPUTER KNOWLEDGE

Lotus 1-2-3	X Stat	Enable
Harvard Graphics	Wordstar	dBase III plus

MEMBERSHIP

American Association of Textile Color and Chemists.   1990–91

JOANNE B. BRIGHT

245 Smith Ave.
Jackson, Mississippi 30309
(222) 898-0987

MEMORIAL HOSPITAL—Jackson, MS   **1991–Present**

Instructional Technologist, Wellness Program   1994–Present

Promote and ensure cost effective utilization of audio visual instructional materials, equipment, and technology throughout the hospital and local community.

- Doubled satellite system utilization.
- Established videotaped in-service/training programs increasing training staff efficiency 100%.
- Videotaped Physician procedures reducing instructional time 60%.
- Introduced and implemented scheduling for training materials, equipment, and facilities eliminating conflicts and increasing utilization 35%.

Wellness Program Facilitator   1992–94

Conceived, developed, and presented Wellness Programs designed to promote healthier lifestyles to Hospital Staff, Community Groups, and Local Employers.

- Established stress, nutrition, and time management–type programs. Achieved 80% continuing attendance.
- Reduced employee stress through development and presentation of staff training programs.
- Refocused underutilized facilities and equipment.

Staff Development Educational Assistant   1991–92

Provided administrative and clerical assistance to staff: dictation, transcribed correspondence, typed instructional materials, scheduled and coordinated training staff/facilities, and conducted stand-up presentations.

JACKSON MISSISSIPPI SCHOOLS   **1981–91**

Educator

Provided instruction at the Community College and High School level on such subjects as: **Secretarial Sciences**, **English**, and **Psychology**.

EDUCATION

MA: University Of Mississippi. Diploma in: Classroom Teaching
Additional Graduate Work in Applied Psychology and Education

BA: Western Mississippi State—Majors and teaching certification in:
English, Literature, and Business Education

AA: Jackson Community College—Diploma in Liberal Arts

CATHLEEN A. WISENHAUSER

643 Jasmine Road   Ann Arbor, MI 48103   (393) 777-9156

BECKENRIDGE CAD/CAM, INC.   **Ann Arbor, MI**

Human Resources Development Specialist   **1993–97**

Responsible for analyzing development/training needs and designing, conducting, and evaluating training programs or retaining outside training resources as appropriate.

- Assisted in design/implementation of technical, field-based training including sales, product, and professional skills.
- Managed technical training program for new college hires.

Personnel Representative   **1991–93**

Supported all levels of personnel in a generalist capacity including: recruiting, employee relations, career counseling, performance appraisals, disciplinary procedures, and writing job descriptions.

- Conducted salary surveys and resolved compensation issues.
- Developed and coordinated standard practices and procedures for company's college relations/recruiting program.
- Supervised one nonexempt employee.
- Represented company at career fairs, professional society functions and awards programs, open houses, etc.

Participated in policy revision, interpretation, and implementation; EEO and affirmative action tracking and record keeping; writing both internal and external informational materials; coordinating company-sponsored activities; and some administering of company benefit program.

Senior Personnel Administrator   **1988–91**

- Coordinated and administered all domestic and international relocations, including policy interpretation and revision.
- Designed and conducted employee relocation survey resulting in more cost-effective procedures and higher employee morale.
- Recruited candidates for all corporate and field nonexempt positions as well as summer internships and part-time positions.
- Promoted from: **Personnel Assistant**. 1986–88

EDUCATION

BS: Sociology/English—Cum Laude—Eastern University—1988

WORKSHOPS/SEMINARS

Instructional Design Workshop

Effective Presentation Skills

The Supervisor as a Member of Management

Effective Classroom Training Techniques

DARLENE D. BIRD

3231 Brandeis Road,   **Hollyfield Hills, CT 88307**   **(913) 851-1936**

FEDERAL-UNITED CORPORATION, Westfield, CT   1975–Present
Administrator, Investor Relations
Liaison between transfer agent (bank) and shareholders. Developed programs to increase public awareness of company. Heavily involved with National Investor Relations Institute (NIRI) and National Association of Investors Corporation (NAIC).

* Developed and presented payroll deduction stock purchase program for hourly employees resulting in 50% plant enrollment.
* Designed fact brochure for customer/shareholder distribution.
* Maintained 50/50 mix of individual and institutional investors through company promotion at NAIC Investor Fairs.

Supervisor, Corporate Financial Reporting Systems
Managed monthly financial consolidation and reporting for Fortune 500 multinational automotive manufacturer/distributor. Coordinated data collection and financial reports. Disseminated information between corporate and manufacturing groups.

Conducted domestic/international software training classes. Selected to implement and debug computerized financial reporting system which resulted in:

* $1,000,000 annual reduction in mainframe charges.
* Elimination of 300+ overtime hours and one exempt position.
* Implementation of telecommunication system resulting in 50% reduction of telex charges.

Accountant/Coordinator, International Financial Reporting
Responsible for monthly financial consolidation and reporting needs. Extensive foreign travel to implement and train personnel on financial reporting software: Micro Control and Quik-Comm.

* Promoted from: **Accounting Clerk**. Administered domestic/foreign ledgers, dividends, royalties, intercompany accounts/billing, accounts receivable/payable, inventory accounting, and Canadian accounting and accounts payable.

EDUCATION
BA–General Studies–Taxon University, Colchester, FL–1991
Minors: Business Administration and Latin American Studies
Third-year level fluency in Spanish.

<u>DARLENE D. BIRD</u>

3231 Brandeis Road,   Hollyfield Hills, CT 88307   (913) 851-1936

FEDERAL-UNITED CORPORATION, Westfield, CT

Administrator, Investor Relations   1992–Present
Liaison between transfer agent (bank) and shareholders. Developed programs to increase public awareness of company. Heavily involved with National Investor Relations Institute (NIRI) and National Association of Investors Corporation (NAIC).

* Developed and presented payroll deduction stock purchase program for hourly employees resulting in 50% plant enrollment.
* Designed fact brochure for customer/shareholder distribution.
* Maintained 50/50 mix of individual and institutional investors through company promotion at NAIC Investor Fairs.

Supervisor, Corporate Financial Reporting Systems   1985–1992
Managed monthly financial consolidation and reporting for Fortune 500 multinational automotive manufacturer/distributor. Coordinated data collection and financial reports. Disseminated information between corporate and manufacturing groups.

Conducted domestic/international software training classes. Selected to implement and debug computerized financial reporting system which resulted in:

* $1,000,000 annual reduction in mainframe charges.
* Elimination of 300+ overtime hours and one exempt position.
* Implementation of telecommunication system resulting in 50% reduction of telex charges.

Accountant/Coordinator, International Financial Reporting
                                                          1980—1985
Responsible for monthly financial consolidation and reporting needs. Extensive foreign travel to implement and train personnel on financial reporting software: Micro Control and Quik-Comm.

* Promoted from: **Accounting Clerk**. Administered domestic/foreign ledgers, dividends, royalties, intercompany accounts/billing, accounts receivable/payable, inventory accounting, and Canadian accounting and accounts payable.

EDUCATION/SEMINARS

BA—General Studies—Taxon University, Colchester, FL—1991
Minors: Business Administration and Latin American Studies
Third-year level fluency in Spanish.

Administrator training: 3-Com, Novell, IBM Token-Ring Networks. Experienced in: Lotus 1-2-3, Harvard Graphics, and WordPerfect.

CONFIDENTIAL

JOHN J. HOLLANDER

20010 San Raphael   Lachmont Village, CA 48076   (121) 456-7899

BULLSEYE CORPORATION—1976–Present
International Headquarters, San Diego, CA

Buyer/Senior Buyer

15 years domestic and import buying experience for nation's third largest mass merchandiser. Extensive travel in, knowledge of, and contacts in Orient markets: **Mainland China, Korea, Japan, Taiwan, Hong Kong,** and **Philippines**. Specific categories have included:

Gloves—Infants through Men's Departments: Fashion, Work, Garden, Hunting, and Ski/Sport.

Umbrellas/Rainwear—Men's, Ladies', and Children's Umbrellas. Ladies', Girls', and Children's Rainwear.

Belts—Ladies' and Children's Belts and Belt Bags.

Wigs—Ladies' synthetic Wigs and Hairpieces.

Established and maintained relationships with major U.S. suppliers and importers. Responsible for developing merchandise lines, styles, colors, and patterns. Experienced in dealing with quotas and customs regulations.

ACCOMPLISHMENTS

- Glove Department volume increased by $18,000,000 from 1979–97. Gross Profit for last five years averaged in excess of 50%.

- Expanded Umbrellas import vendor base from single Taiwanese maker to include makers in Hong Kong, Indonesia, and China. Volume increase 1987–97 averaged $950,000 per year. Gross Profit averaged in excess of 54% over same period.

- Belt Department volume increased by $7,000,000 from 1984–97. Responsible for department exclusive of 1988–90.

ADDITIONAL RESPONSIBILITIES

- Financial planning for individual departments: Inventory Levels, Receivings, Mark Downs, Gross Profit Percent and Dollars, and Turnover by month for total year.

- Plot Planning/Plan-O-Grams for Departments and Division.

- Selection and coordination of merchandise for ad programs.

- Domestic/Overseas Buy Plans and Merchandise Reviews.

John J. Hollander
(page 2 of 2)

- Planning/presenting merchandise displays for National Seminars.
- Hands-on computer experience in financial/ladder plans.

OTHER POSITIONS HELD

Regional Manager—Fashion Accessories, Central Region, Sooner, OK

Regional Manager—Fashion Accessories, Prairie States Region, Kansas City, MO
Assistant Regional Manager

Planner—Drapery/Window Treatments, San Diego, CA

PRIOR EXPERIENCE
Browns, Missouri/Kansas Division   1969–76

Buyer—Notions, Cameras, Carpets, Rugs, Oriental Rugs

Associate Buyer—Ladies' Coats and Suits

Assistant Buyer—Men's Furnishings

Area Supervisor—Ladies' Apparel, Men's, Cosmetics, Stationery, Books, and
                         Notions

Store Manager—Independence, MO

Operations Manager—Topeka, KS

MILITARY HISTORY

U.S. Army Reserve. 1963–69. Specialist 5th Class. Vietnam Veteran. Vietnam
Service Medal, Army Commendation Medal, Good Conduct Medal. Honorable
Discharge.

EDUCATION

B.S., Business Administration. University of Kansas, Lawrence, KS. Graduated
1963.

RAYMOND STROM, JR.

763 N. Long Lake Road
National City, NV 88900
(998) 456-6543

COREOMATIC, SALCRAFT DIVISION—Wendell, IA

Plant Manager   1988–97

Managed 22,000 sq. ft., 45 employees, facility manufacturing High Speed Steel and Carbide cutting tools. Shipped $1.2 Million—$3.4 Million annually. Managed one Superintendent, six Department Leaders, and Quality Control Inspector. Duties included overseeing Engineering, Estimating, and all manufacturing departments; hiring personnel; and establishing safety and plant cleanliness policies.

- Increased plant capacity through introduction of group meetings aimed at reducing "time per piece."
- Introduced MRP II shop floor control for tracking work in progress.
- Reduced scrap and rework 50% through monitoring program.
- Cut run-time 30% through implementation of CNC cutter-grinder.

Plant Superintendent   1987–88

Responsible for plant manufacturing including: Quality, Maintenance, Shipping Departments, and Manufacturing areas. Established/monitored shipping goals.

- Developed follow-up system for job location.
- Set goals, increased shipment from $70,000 to $220,000 per month.
- Eliminated janitorial position with "do-it-yourself" program.
- OSHA inspections produced 0 penalties.

Foreman   1983–87

Monitored all manufacturing departments and instituted leader meetings to plan shipments. Led employee evaluation sessions utilizing daily department performance logs.

Production Leader 1979–83/Lathe Hand 1977–79

EDUCATION

Machine Shop Practice, Mellton State Technical—Tuscoloosa, AL
College Prep, Oscalusa High School—Oscalusa, IA

IN-HOUSE SEMINARS:

Managing Employee Relations, Coreomatic Management   1995
Professional Communication, Coreomatic Management   1995
JIT for America, Ken Wantuck & Associates   1994
Problem Solving, Coreomatic Management   1993

ADULT EDUCATION:

Deaf Employee Communication (Sign Language)   1985

RONALD L. BAILEY

20280 Keyline Drive   **(777) 369-1393**
Athens, GA 47234   **(777) 362-2187**

Production Supervisor
BBB, INC., Southern Heights, GA 1990–Present

Supervise Forging department for the Steering and Suspension Division facility of this multinational manufacturer of automotive and aerospace supplies. Department consists of up to 48 hourly, UAW employees. Duties and responsibilities include:

- Organize, schedule, and delegate work assignments.
- Interface with group leaders and machine operators to achieve peak operating efficiency.
- Research and handle union grievances.
- Communicate company policy, procedures, and related changes to subordinates maintaining effective employee relations and communications.
- Prepare and submit daily production reports.
- Implement, supervise, and maintain safety programs.
- Read blueprints and inspect parts to ensure strict adherence to production standards and specifications.

Additional duties and responsibilities: ordering stock daily, monitoring cost and quality control, training new employees, and recommending new ideas.

Forging Operator. 1984–90. **Promoted.**

Miscellaneous Operator. 1979–84. **Promoted.**

EDUCATION: Southern Heights High School. 1978.

Southern Heights College: Management classes.

BBB, Inc. Classes: **Statistical Process Control, Advanced Management, Dynamic Supervision, Health and Safety.**

PERSONAL: Willing to relocate.

References Furnished Upon Request

WILLIAM B. COHEN

1123 Evans Court   ∘   **Fort Wayne, IN 89815**   ∘   **(219) 486-3570**

UNLIMITED TECHNOLOGIES CORPORATION. Alexander Standard.
Midwest Division, 1994–Present

Quality Assurance Manager
Member of six-person division staff supporting three plants engaged in the manufacture of natural and LP gas controls for domestic/foreign, consumer/industrial use. Directly responsible for total quality program including reliability testing. Also act as Quality Control Manager at Auburn, IN facility supervising five salaried personnel. Accomplishments:

- Reviewed/revised all major quality documents and data collection forms.
- Established monthly QC report summaries through introduction of computerized documentation system.
- Computerized vendor quality history reporting.
- Upgraded dimensional inspection equipment to: electronic digital readout, geometric functions, and statistical process control outputs. Also upgraded microprocessor controlled production test equipment increasing accuracy and dependability.
- Wrote job descriptions and hired QC engineers for key positions.

UNLIMITED TECHNOLOGIES CORPORATION. Alexander Standard.
Eastern Division, 1992–94

Senior QC Engineer
Developed quality program for commercial and military aircraft environmental systems. Monitored production initiating corrective action as required.

- Given design engineering authority for disposition of nonconforming material.
- Initiated computerized customer return reporting and analysis system.

TORIN CORPORATION. Information Systems Division, 1989–92

Quality Control Supervisor
Directed quality program at Torrington, CT plant supervising two salaried employees and 13 bargaining unit inspectors.

CAROLL GLASS WORKS. Industrial Products Division, 1987–89

Quality Control Engineer
Responsible for QC lab, all production gauging systems, and precision glass tooling. Supervised seven of 30 inspectors.

MILITARY HISTORY

U.S. Marine Corps.

1986–87. **Captain.** Company Commander responsible for $7,000,000+ of armored equipment including administrative maintenance, logistics, communication, and motor transport assets. Supervised six officers and 250 enlisted personnel.

1986. **Company Executive Officer.** Second in command.

1981–85. **2nd/1st Lieutenant.** Battalion staff.

EDUCATION

U.S. Naval Academy. Annapolis, MD. B.S. Operations Analysis. Graduated 1981.

PROFESSIONAL MEMBERSHIP

American Society for Quality Control

DONALD E. LENHARDT

1356 Joanne	Grassville, IA 48220-2320	213-546-0094

REHABILITATION CENTER, Detroit, MI   **1991–96**

CLIENT SERVICE MANAGER—(1995–96)

Supervised department of five. Directed Center for Independent Living's work with 50 agencies and six governmental departments coordinating Wayne County's physically handicapped services. Coordinated programming, admissions, and marketing.

- Administered CIL funds, grants, payroll, and petty cash.
- Wrote seven program proposals—creation of new housing options, development of funding sources, co-op programs.
- Created education/advocacy programs for the severely handicapped. Quarterbacked handicapped forums. Linked clients' legal services. Worked closely with city and county officials.

DIRECTOR—(1991–95)

Program, Administrative, and Budgetary responsibility supervising four-member staff. Developed funding. Served as national, state, and local disabled persons advocate.

- Wrote and presented agency funding proposals.
- Implemented TV, radio, and print marketing and public relations.
- Negotiated third-party fee schedules.

HOLY GRAIL HOSPITAL, Southfield, MI   **1985–91**

MENTAL HEALTH TECHNICIAN

Provided group/individual counseling. Supervised community college Mental Health major. Wrote psychiatric hospital program proposals.

GREENTREE HOSPITAL, Ferndale, MI   **1982–85**

MENTAL HEALTH WORKER

Provided group and individual counseling to adolescents and adults in a psychiatric hospital.

UNITED INDUSTRIES' ASSOCIATION, Chicago, IL   **1979–82**

DIRECTOR

Directed thriving $400,000 per year nonprofit agency charged with meeting community needs. Developed funding. Interacted with the Chicago School System. Created and coordinated teenage educational work experience program. Supervised "Meals-on-Wheels."

EDUCATION/CERTIFICATION

MA: Management & Supervision—Central Iowa University—1985

BA: Psychology—Iowa State University—1979

Social Worker—State of Iowa

RONALD F. LEWIS

3954 Meadowbrook Drive, Troy, IA 88084   (414) 528-2976/(414) 362-2187

DIRECTOR, CORPORATE PURCHASING
Prime Meat Food Products Corporation, Des Moines, IA
Responsible for $60MM annual budget for major meat packer. Supervise 6 plant and corporate Purchasing Managers. Duties/responsibilities include: procurement of capital assets, ingredients, processing, and packaging supplies.

- Negotiated annual shipping container contracts reducing costs 18%. Formed vendor-user cost reduction team resulting in $10,000 savings.
- Interfaced with Graphic Arts Designer and printers to control print quality and costs for variety of packaging materials.
- Standardized annual packaging supply requirements and obtained vendor pricing guarantees reducing costs 30%.
- Initiated Profit Improvement Incentive Program saving $500,000+ through reduction of supply inventories.
- Authored purchasing policies and procedures controlling unauthorized capital equipment expenditures.

Introduced written specifications for processing/packaging supplies. Standardized supply item descriptions. Developed Machine Operator Training Program facilitating introduction of co-extruded packaging technology.

SPECIAL ASSISTANT TO PRESIDENT/OWNER
Sweetie Meat Pies, Inc., Troy, IA
Established and implemented company operations system for specialty meat products retailer with 100 outlets. System included: raw materials and finished goods inventory control, sales/marketing control, and purchasing requisition/ordering.

- Initiated and implemented Managerial Training Program for store managers.
- Selected and established corporate office location. Supervised space allocation and modifications, procurement of equipment and furnishings, and installation of computer and communications systems.

VICE PRESIDENT AND GENERAL MANAGER
Parkview Village Apartments, Westville, MA
Responsible for administration of 600 unit garden apartment complex. Duties and responsibilities included: supervising rental, security, maintenance personnel. Directed construction activities. Initiated renter inspection agreement form reducing maintenance costs 30%.

PURCHASING ADVISOR
First Bank and Trust, Baltimore, MD

Advised Purchasing Department of major Maryland banking institution. Planned, developed, and wrote Purchasing Policies & Procedures Manual. Reduced costs of printed forms by 25%.

MANAGER OF PURCHASING
Darton Company, Baltimore, MD

Controlled all purchasing activities for bank holding company with 13 member banks. Wrote procedures manual. Negotiated banking equipment procurement contracts reducing costs 20%. Also negotiated contracts for acquisition of future bank site properties. Supervised the purchasing, office administration, inventory control, and record retention of all banks.

EDUCATION

UNIVERSITY OF DELAWARE. B.S. Degree, Industrial Management, 1979

ASSOCIATIONS

National Association of Purchasing Managers

Vice President, French-American Congress

PERSONAL

Willing to relocate. Speak German, Russian, French, and Polish.

FERDINAND J. REIMEREZ

21 Lakeview Drive, Apt. #10   **(713) 362-2187**
Beavertown, Wisconsin 48198   **(713) 487-5864**

EDUCATION: **B.B.A., Production & Operations Management.** 1994
University of Wisconsin—Whitewater, WI
Related Courses: Production Planning and Control, Inventory Planning, Manufacturing Processes, Material Flow, Management of Service Operations, Cobol and Fortran Programming, Information Systems Management.

EXPERIENCE: Frisbee Food Company, Allen Park, WI 1994–95
Production Supervisor for a leading manufacturer and distributor of snack foods. Supervised union workgroups of 4–25 employees and up to 4 product lines at plant with 600+ employees. Duties and responsibilities included:

- Scheduling crews on a daily basis.
- Monitoring production to meet 99% service-to-sales compliance rate.
- Controlling raw materials inventories.
- Training and developing personnel.
- Handling union grievances.
- Coordinating interdepartmental safety program.

Submitted method improvements resulting in $20,000 savings. Interfaced daily with equipment operators and maintenance personnel to ensure peak machinery efficiency.

Intern Production Analyst—Beloit, WI. Summer, 1993. Assigned to assist various production departments while attending college. Filled in for vacations.

OTHER POSITIONS: **Security Guard**—Safeguard Protective, Milwaukee, WI Part Time, 1991–93.

Ski Lift Operator—Frosty Valley Resort, Easton, WI Seasonal, 1989–94.

MEMBERSHIPS: American Production and Inventory Control Society

Membership Chairperson—Alumni and Fundraising Committee

Management Games, Team Member

J. JOHNSON JACKSON III

1001 Wadsworth   **(919) 646-8173**
Birmingham, AL 68010   **(919) 362-2187**

OBJECTIVE: Industrial Engineering position concentrating on: Layouts, Projects, Material Handling, and Capital Justification.

EDUCATION: • B.S.I.E., University of Alabama. 1982.

• Supercalc, Multimate. IBM PC Seminars. 1999.

• CAD/CAM Seminar and Training. SCS Inc. 1997.

• Electrical Blueprint/Circuits Course. Tri-Land Engineering College. 1996.

EMPLOYER: SCS INC., Birmingham, AL. 1982–Present.

INDUSTRIAL ENGINEERING EXPERIENCE

Layout/Methods. Created Office and Manufacturing layouts for 500,000 sq. ft. plant utilizing IBM CAD/CAM system. Involved in production area consolidation & construction of 48,000 sq. ft. additional office/lab space. Member of value analysis team responsible for relocating equipment, facilitating and simplifying material handling—resulted in $60,000 per year manpower savings. Worked directly with management renovating existing office space due to introduction of modular furniture.

Projects. Experienced in all types of projects; from $2,500 equipment relocation to coordinating $400,000 machine overhaul program. Areas of expertise include:

• Researching and evaluating technical data.
• Developing required layouts.
• Writing project descriptions and estimating related costs.
• Formulating projects and obtaining approvals.
• Working with Purchasing, Vendors, Management, and Skilled Trades.

Budget/Estimating. Evaluated costs associated with proposed product engineering changes. Also responsible for estimating new parts manufacturing cost and establishing fiscal year budget rate sheets.

Time Study. Conducted stopwatch time studies, random samplings, and delay studies. Trained and skilled in Methods Time Measurement.

Member: American Institute of Plant Engineers

SUSAN B. KAHN

126 Longlake Boulevard
Dawson City, TX 99017
(523) 335-2080

REPRESENTATIVE PROFESSIONAL ACCOMPLISHMENTS

- As Chairman of Oakwood County Community Development Advisory Council, during 1987 and 1988, administered Block Grant federal funds and program income amounting to $7,509,742.
- Responsible for $46,104,000 budget (20% of $241,359,000 Oakwood County budget), while serving as the Chairman of Health and Human Services Committee. Matching state and federal funds increases budget of county programs to $251,200,000.
- In capacity as Chairman, Health and Human Services Committee, direct reports include Public Health, Mental Health, Medical Examiner, Camp Oakwood, Children's Village, Medical Care Facility, Department of Social Services, Oakwood Livingston Human Service Agency, Probate Court, and Area Agency for Aging.
- While Chairman of Community Development Advisory Council, reviewed applications and encouraged private sector partnerships through Commercial Assistance Program (CAP) which allowed leveraging of $700,000 into $3,100,000.

PROFESSIONAL EXPERIENCE

OAKWOOD COUNTY BOARD OF COMISSIONERS (1982–Present)
District 12 Commissioner
Elected Office serving Oakwood, Bray, Royal Pine, and Byrne, TX.

HOLIDAY FARE DEPARTMENT STORE COMPANY (1968–88)

Senior Corporate Shortage Auditor	(1986–88)
Corporate Shortage Auditor	(1983–85)
Merchandise Manager	(1975–82)
Assistant Buyer/Associate Buyer	(1968–74)

EDUCATION

BS: Economics/Business Administration, Wesley College, 1968.

RELATED ACTIVITIES

Frequent guest speaker to community/business/service groups
Officer: Oakwood County Business & Professionals Club
Columnist for *Bray Oakwood Gazette* since January 1984
Member: Bray and Royal Pine Chambers of Commerce
Officer: OJWC—Oakwood Junior Women's Club

CLEMENT T. BROWN

2233 North Liverpool Road
Winchester Hills, MI 48064

Office: (303) 399-2187
Home: (303) 699-2832

SALES/MARKETING MANAGEMENT

JOHNSON, World Headquarters, Troy, MI 1978–Present
Extensive sales/marketing managerial experience with industry leader in the design, manufacture, and sales of hydraulic and electronic control systems. Commercial, worldwide operations involve $400MM annual sales and 4,500 employees. Positions:

Market/Product Planning Manager; Market Engineer; Product Manager; Area Sales, Sales Engineer.

MARKETING
Duties and responsibilities have included managing 15-person department with $1MM budget: salaries, travel, and product prototypes, and developing concise, long-range marketing plans. Also . . .

- Directed $40MM product line with 18% ROS.
- Planned 20% cost reduction for $10MM product.
- Supervised automotive plant specifications activity.

SALES
Experience includes managing $30MM annual sales through 20 outside sales people and 7 District Sales Offices. Recruited and hired sales engineers.

- Negotiated three exclusive source contracts worth $4MM.
- Closed $3.5MM annual purchase agreement.
- Solved delivery problem with innovative purchase contract.
- Planned and conducted national sales meeting involving 90 participants.

ENGINEERING
Background includes designing hydraulic systems to meet specific requirements and involved direct customer interface. Developed handling motion equations for articulated vehicles. Experienced in computer modeling and vehicle parts design.

EDUCATION: MSE University of Michigan, 1991

MBA Michigan State University, 1986

BME General Motors Institute, 1970

Chapter 3

How to Write Attention-Grabbing Cover Letters

W hen you mail your resume, you will also write a cover letter to accompany it. Not only does such a letter introduce
you to the reader, but it also strengthens your bid for the
position in question. Just like a resume, the cover letter must cry out,
"Read Me! Read Me!"

Think of the cover letter as a delicious appetizer that introduces the entrée. It must delight and excite the palate. It must
exclaim to the reader, "If you think *this* is great, just wait until
you taste what follows!"

Cover letters that open, "To Whom It May Concern," followed by, "I saw your ad, here's my resume," are like a limp salad.
Instead of turning the reader on, they turn him or her off.
Another real turnoff? Job hunters that mail out bushels of
resumes all accompanied by a form cover letter. What do *you* do
when you receive mail like this? So do they!

Unless you have contacted the employer by phone, the cover
letter is the first sales piece to greet his or her eyes. As a sales piece

it must burst out of the chute with both guns blazing. Never forget that everything you do in your job search is done with the thought of selling yourself to an employer. And so it is and must be with a cover letter. Because it is often the first thing read by the employer it must really sell or you might never make it to phase two, the reading of your resume.

Don't ever make the mistake of belittling the importance of a cover letter. Because most job seekers write such poor, misdirected letters, yours can assume even greater importance when well written—and, *directed to the decision maker.*

If you are like most people, you probably dread writing cover letters. I know exactly how you feel. I used to dread it, too. And I have helped job seekers write them daily for years! Trying to find something intelligent and directly applicable to the job in question can be difficult. But, fear not. If you have already assembled a wealth of sales-oriented accomplishments and achievements a formerly dreaded task becomes acceptable, even challenging.

W3SP—The Standard Cover Letter Format

W3SP is my formula to follow for facilitating cover letter writing. It stands for the 3 W's—**WHO, WHY, WHAT,** and your **Sales Pitch (SP)**. Let's take a look at how easy it is to write a cover letter using the W3SP formula.

The first thing that appears at the top of your letter is your letterhead. I like the following format, but you can do as you please as long as it looks attractive and businesslike.

YOUR NAME

Street Address   City, State, and Zip Code   Phone Number(s)

Skip about three or four lines and type, also margin left:

Date

Skip two more lines and type in the contact information. This is the first **W** in **W3SP**, the **WHO** part of the formula telling who you are writing to. Make every effort to obtain the decision maker's name, spelled correctly, and his or her correct title:

Contact's Name
Title
Company Name
Street
City, State, and Zip Code.

Next, skip three lines and type in the salutation:

Dear Mr. Descoteaux:

If you cannot uncover the contact's name and title, skip four lines instead of three and launch right into the letter. A meaningless salutation such as "Dear Advertiser" does nothing to enhance the saleability of your material. How do you feel when you receive mail addressed to "Dear Friend" or to "Postal Patron"? There is nothing difficult about following this cover letter format. The toughest thing to do is get the name of the right person to write to, the decision maker.

Now for the opening, or introductory paragraph. Tell the reader **WHY** you're writing to him or her. For example, if you're answering an ad:

Dear Mr. Descoteaux:

I am interested in the Accounting Manager position advertised in the November 18 *Richfield Ledger*. A resume is enclosed for your review.

If you've spoken to someone prior to writing:

Thank you for taking the time to discuss the Accounting Manager's position with me. Here is the resume you requested.

Try to avoid cliches such as, "Enclosed please find my resume." (Oh, was it lost?) Or, "I have enclosed my resume per your request." Write like you speak, but be careful to maintain a businesslike tone.

Just tell the reader **WHY** you are writing. That's it. That's all it takes to write the opening **WHY** paragraph.

Let's skip down a couple of paragraphs to the concluding paragraph—the **WHAT** paragraph. Here's where you tell the reader **WHAT** to expect next. Typically, it is something like this:

I'll call next week to make certain you received my resume. In the meantime, if you have any questions, you may reach me at 313-123-4321. Thank you for your consideration.

Then, skip two spaces and type:

Sincerely,

Leave five or six blank lines for writing your signature. Directly below your signature type your name.

Your Signature
Your Name

All that is missing now is a paragraph or two sandwiched in between the opening and closing paragraphs. You've supplied the bread for the sandwich. Now it's time to fill it with something tasty and appealing.

It's time for your **SALES PITCH**. This is the most important part of your letter. It's time to tell the reader why he or she should continue to read your letter and why he or she should invite you in for an interview as quickly as possible. It's time to make the reader look forward to reading your resume to see what other great stuff you have to offer.

For example, you might start with an opening sentence or two like this:

> I have three years' experience using Lotus 1-2-3, as called for in the help wanted ad. In fact, my background includes conducting several Lotus 1-2-3 training sessions for entry level accounting personnel. Additionally, I have:
>
> • Created and implemented a cost-accounting system, saving the company 3 hours of bookkeeping time per week.
>
> • Detected and rectified a clerical error that would have resulted in a $10,000 monthly debit.
>
> • Received a letter of commendation from the company president for service above and beyond the line of duty.

Finally, you conclude with the **WHAT** paragraph. **WHAT** do you want to happen next? **WHAT** can he or she expect to happen next?

> You can expect me to give you a call. I want to make certain you received my resume. Thank you once again for your consideration.

W3SP. If you keep this formula in mind you shouldn't have any problems composing attention-getting cover letters. It follows a very natural sequence: **WHO** you are writing to, **WHY** you are writing, the **SALES PITCH** that will make the person get excited about what you can do for his or her company, and **WHAT** can or will be expected to happen as a result of this contact.

Standard Cover Letter

YOUR NAME

Street   City/State   Phone #(s)

Date

Contact's Name
Title
Company Name
Street
City, State, Zip Code

Dear Mr. Descoteaux:

Your ad in the November 18 *Richfield Ledger* for an Accounting Manager interests me. A resume is enclosed for your review.

I have three years' experience using Lotus 1-2-3, as called for in your ad. In fact, my background includes conducting Lotus 1-2-3 training sessions for entry level accounting personnel. Additionally, I have:

- Created and implemented a cost-accounting system, saving the company 3 hours of bookkeeping time per week.
- Detected and rectified a clerical error that would have resulted in a $10,000 monthly debit.
- Received a letter of commendation from the company president for service above and beyond the line of duty.

You can expect me to give you a call. I want to make certain you received my resume. Thank you for your consideration.

Sincerely,

Signature

Name

The Two-Column Format

The two-column format makes it easy for the reader to see exactly how close you come to meeting the requirements given in his or her ad. (Naturally, you wouldn't select this format if what you have to offer doesn't come close to the job requirements.)The two-column cover letter also works well when your qualifications meet or exceed the requirements for the position. The key, as in all of your employer contacts, is to try to make what you have to offer just what the reader needs.

As I indicated, the two-column format is especially appropriate when you know your qualifications are exactly or almost exactly what the employer wants.

The Mini-Proposal

Sometimes it is possible to initiate employer interest when there is no specific job opening. One way to do this is through a mini-proposal letter.

The mini-proposal is just what the name implies, a brief proposal designed to stimulate interest and lead to more fruitful discussions. The idea is to use your background and experience to get your foot in the door.

You can use the mini-proposal tactic to try to interest the employer in some type of consulting or temporary employment arrangement. This can be especially effective if the employer has a "freeze" on hiring. It may present him or her with a way to end-run this condition.

Approaches to Use in Writing Mini-Proposals

1. Surprise Approach—A mini-proposal can assume the surprise approach. It is mailed to the appropriate company contact without advance warning.
2. Query Approach—The mini-proposal may be mailed to the appropriate party after having broached the idea with him or her and received a positive response.
3. After Interview Approach—A mini-proposal can be used as a follow-up after an interview when it looks like there is

Two-Column Cover Letter

YOUR NAME

Street   Town/City   Telephone #(s)

Date

Contact's Name
Title
Company Name
Street
City, State, Zip Code

Dear Mr. Descoteaux:

I am interested in the Accounting Manager position advertised in the November 18 *Richfield Ledger*. A resume is enclosed for your review.

Your Requirements	My Qualifications
• Associate Degree or its equivalent.	• Business Degree from Bay State Business School.
• Five years' invoicing experience.	• Six years' invoicing experience.
• Familiarity with Lotus 1-2-3.	• Have taught Lotus 1-2-3 classes.

You can expect me to give you a call. I want to make certain you received my resume. Thank you once again for your consideration.

Sincerely,

Signature

Name

interest in you, but not quite enough to win the day. It is an attempt to breathe new life into your candidacy.

A mini-proposal follows all the rules associated with any effective cover letter. It is concise, inviting to read, and meticulously crafted to sell your qualifications. It adheres to the W3SP formula.

Unlike most cover letters, the mini-proposal ventures into untested but promising waters. It must be diplomatically couched because it presents your idea and not the employer's. If it leads the employer to think that it *is* his or her idea, fine. Ideally, the reader should exclaim aloud, "That's a wonderful idea!"

Unlike a resume, the mini-proposal often falls or stands on its own merits. It doesn't delve deeply into your past history but tells only what would interest the reader. Like any good cover letter, it leaves the reader wanting to know more.

If you can, include some appealing and supportive information to give credence to your suggestion. Think about including such items as news articles, company reports, competitor's sales literature, or articles about the competition. If this supporting material is graphic in nature all the better, especially if it is in color.

The Motivator

Occasionally, you will encounter a situation where the interviewer obviously is impressed by you but seems reluctant to make a commitment. There are many reasons why this may be so. He or she may be having a difficult time obtaining hiring permission from his or her boss, have become temporarily embroiled in an internal issue, have suddenly been given a higher priority assignment, or have been called out of town on company business.

Whatever the reason, waiting to see when and if you will be offered the position can drive you crazy. Should you run into such a predicament, here is an approach you should consider taking.

Write a motivator. A motivator is a letter that, diplomatically, with a sense of urgency, reminds the reader your future is in his hands; you really do want to work for him, but you can't afford to sit around much longer awaiting his decision. It reminds him he must commit to some sort of positive action, and soon, if he really wants you to become a member of his team.

Mini-Proposal—Example 1

ELIZABETH M. SAGE
23 Severance Lane   Outplacement, AZ 54321 (412) 908-2212

October 19,1997

Mr. Jeffrey Hurst
Vice President
Marigold Products, Inc.
896 Hurley Circle
Southfield, MI 48075

Dear Jeff,

   Bruce Hitchcock advised me on Tuesday that a policy position has been taken to prohibit all hiring at Marigold Products, Inc. This is obviously a disappointment to me.

   I am confident, however, that you could use my skills to contribute quickly and significantly to the profitability of your jibbit business while still adhering to company policy. By creating a consulting relationship we could improve current operational results and establish confidence in each other to facilitate a long-term relationship when corporate policy permits.

   I will contact your Northfield office the week of October 24 to learn your reaction to this proposed course of action.

Best regards,

Betty Sage

Betty Sage

Mini-Proposal—Example 2

CHARLES RAYMOND GONFLINGER
1926 Broadway Circle, Opelika, AL 87689
O:(234)475-2388 H:(234)555-9009

December 2, 1997

Jane E. Littlefield
Vice President Operations
Big Deal Enterprises
1111 Maxwell Building, Ste. 10
Canterbury, CT 29385

Dear Ms. Littlefield:

As the number of airlines has decreased through mergers and acquisitions, fares have increased. In fact, today's air fares are almost as high as they were before deregulation.

A top-notch corporate travel director, however, can help to save an employer incredible amounts of money if discount opportunities are fully explored. Although I do not have any reason to believe your company has a current situation available for someone with my credentials, let me recommend how you could realize substantial savings within your corporate travel budget:

- Choose a Discount Airline. Their cost of flying averages about 6 cents per passenger mile, compared with about 9 cents for other carriers. By the way, I know the best discount airlines.
- Fly Competitive Routes. Fares on multiple-airline routes are much cheaper than on routes controlled by one or two major carriers. Stop flying nonstop on non-competitive routes, break trips into two competitive flights and SAVE. It just so happens that I know these competitive routes backwards and forwards.
- Fly to Less Popular Nearby Airports. From there take ground transportation to the final destination. Even renting limos to reach the final destination will result in some

---

very impressive cost savings over the air fare to well-known and heavily traveled airports. Your executives would probably enjoy the chance to relax in a limo on the way to business meetings . . . don't you agree? (Incidentally, I've made a very careful study of 47 less-popular nearby airports, and I have discovered none located more than 30 miles from the nearest major airport.)

I will call early next week to see if it would make sense for us to get together.

Sincerely,

Charles Gonflinger

Charles Gonflinger

Bear in mind, whatever you write has to be diplomatically stated. It has to promote a sense of urgency on your behalf. It should show that you are sincerely interested in working for both the company and the interviewer. It might also contain the slightest hint of apology for putting the reader on the spot.

Dave, one of my clients, was close to landing a controller's position but he could not get the decision maker to make a definite commitment. Although there wasn't an opening at present, Dave knew the employer was anxious to replace an ineffectual controller with someone new. In this instance, the decision maker was the president of the company so Dave knew that whether or not he was to be hired lay directly in this person's hands.

Dave could feel this, his one and only big opportunity, slipping away. Although he felt uncomfortable doing so, he began calling the employer to remind him he was still very interested in the job and to maintain a high profile. He couldn't get through to the president, and his calls went unanswered. And so, reluctantly, he sat down and wrote a motivator.

Dave's motivator letter did exactly what it was intended to do. It aroused anxiety in the president, who really did want to hire him. Fearful he might lose him, he called him in and hired him as an assistant-to-the-president until he could bring himself to release the present controller and place Dave in the post.

To his credit, Dave sat down and skillfully composed the following letter. You'll seldom find a better motivator. After he was hired, Dave discovered the former controller was a longtime employee of the company and a close personal friend of the president.

The Resuscitator

You've had a very promising interview. You are one of the finalists for the position. You anxiously await the decision. Then it arrives . . . close, but no cigar. They have selected another candidate. What do you do? Curl up in a corner and cry?

That's what other job seekers might do, *but not you*. You really wanted that job. Didn't you? Now is not the time to take "no" for an answer. You know what the sales pros say? "The selling doesn't really begin until you receive a 'No.'"

The Motivator

DAVID ROBERT BARTLETT
9 Huntington Way, Detroit, MI, 48445
O:(313)545/1254 H:(313)522/6776

June 23, 1997

Dear Bill:

Just a brief note to let you know I'm still very interested in the administrative position and working for you. I tried to contact you earlier this week to get an update and see if there's anything I can do to help you bring this process to a close.

I realize you have many pressing matters that require your daily attention, and I'm sure the unpleasant task of having to replace one of your staff is not at the top of the list of things you have, or want, to do. However, the sooner this matter is resolved the sooner you'll get the help you need and expect from this position.

I also want to advise you that since we last met, I've had a number of interviews and have been asked back for a second and final interview this Thursday afternoon. Although my first desire is to work for you, as you are aware, I am not in a position to refuse a legitimate offer without any commitment to me on your part.

Bill, I'm truly excited about this position and the challenge and opportunity it presents. I am very confident that given the chance I will do an outstanding job. I know you won't be disappointed in my desire or work ethics.

Bill, please let me know if there is anything I can do to help bring this to a conclusion. I look forward to hearing from you.

Sincerely,

Dave Bartlett

Dave Bartlett

There are two means of trying to breath new life into an apparently dead job search: phone or write to the employer. Or, better yet, both. My recommendation? Pick up the phone and call the employer.

> Nancy? This is Charlie Smith. Do you have just a minute or two?

> Nancy, I was really looking forward to working with you. As much as I regret your decision, I respect it and don't expect you to change it. I'm just calling to thank you for your consideration and for the time you spent with me.

> Perhaps you might be kind enough to suggest an area or two I might improve in so as to strengthen my job search skills. Any suggestions, no matter how small, would really be welcomed. After all, I do have a job search to get on with.

Now, pause and listen closely to her feedback. Take brief notes. Ask for clarification or suggestions for improvement. But, for goodness sake, don't get into an argument with her. Try to be objective and open-minded. If you don't agree with her perspective let it go.

The resuscitator provides a wonderful opportunity to improve your job search skills. How else can you discover how employers may be viewing your candidacy? There are a few more reasons, besides self-improvement, for soliciting this vital information.

When you use the resuscitator:

- You show the employer that you are ready, willing, and able to improve yourself. Definitely a nice trait for any potential employee to possess.
- You don't just disappear into the sunset. You make a sudden unexpected appearance. You're no quitter; another nice trait for a potential employee to possess.
- You show that you really did appreciate the time the employer spent with you. And, although you're a runner-up, you are a true class act. Yet another nice trait for a potential employee to possess.

The resuscitator is yet another form of written communication that is virtually unused by job seekers. You can really stand out when you write such a letter.

The Resuscitator

GLORIA ALICE WILDFLOWER
44 Marigold Lane, Hawthorne, New Jersey 01234
(514) 998-0987

September 24, 1997

Ms. Flora Bunda
HR Manager
Rosewood Gardens
565 Morninglory
Hawthorne, NJ 01235

Dear Ms. Bunda:

Thanks for taking the time to speak with me on the phone yesterday. I really appreciate your helping me to "get my act together" for future interviews. Your suggestion that I spend some time developing my listening skills will not go unheeded. The next time we talk you will discover that you have my full attention.

Please keep me in mind for future employment with Rosewood. I know I can significantly contribute to your department—especially in the compensation and benefits area.

Another area I could provide some immediate assistance with is labor mediation. As you might recall, I had a great deal of positive experience in this field while at Johnson & McGann. I don't envy you what you are going through right now. If you need any help at all (on or off the payroll) in winning a non-union vote in the upcoming election don't hesitate to give me a call.

Incidentally, I contacted Bill Weaver as you suggested. We are getting together next Monday for an informal meeting. I'll be certain to convey your best wishes to him.

Thanks once again. I'll keep you posted on how things are going. I'm sure your input will bring my job search to an earlier happy ending. Please remember, I'm available if you need me.

Sincerely,

Gloria Wildflower

Gloria Wildflower

The Broadcast Letter

The broadcast letter is a perfect example of the "shotgun" versus the "rifle" approach. It's mailed out, along with your resume, to as many prospective employers as possible. Then you sit back and hope, by virtue of sheer volume, to receive a response.

Typically, broadcast-letter senders address the reader with such endearing salutations as "Dear Sir or Madam" and the equally endearing "To Whom It May Concern." Obviously, this is not the ideal greeting!

If you decide to try the numbers game and send out broadcast letters, at least try to mail them to specific people or titles. For example:

June 1, 1999

Accounting Department Supervisor
Reimer Sisters Accounting Services
78 Aditup Drive, Suite #6758
Ware, MA 00123

As you may have heard, Target Accounting Services has gone out of business. I am forced to seek reemployment. My resume is enclosed, but I would like to present a few highlights from my 12 years with the company.

I received five promotions in four years, working my way up from order entry clerk to Assistant Accounting Supervisor.

...and so on and so forth.

Notice that because the writer did not have a specific name to direct her letter to, she eliminated the salutation altogether and launched right into the letter itself. What's the point of starting with, "Dear Sir or Madam" or "To Whom It May Concern"? The reader will just skim over it anyway.

Broadcast letters are notoriously ineffective. Expect little more than a three to four percent response, with half of these being polite "thank you, but no thanks" form letters. However, even a response this minimal beats waiting around the house hoping to win the lottery. If you should land your new job via this medium be proud. You'll have entered the ranks of the very few who did.

Job seekers in some occupations can use a little more creativity when seeking work than most of us can. This is evidenced by

The Broadcast Letter

MARTIN HOWARD GREENWALL

123 Benton Harbor Drive   Office: 617/898/0090
Benton Harbor, Ml 48909   Home: 617/898/8787

February 1, 1999

Mr. Wallace C. Little
President
Superior Foods
111 Good Food Drive
Indianapolis, IN 12345

Dear Mr. Little:

There's a business in your portfolio that needs help. That's the one I want to work on.

I have over seventeen years of consumer products experience. Ten years with Proctor & Wright. Over six years with McHugh's Chowders. Marketing and general management.

I turned around one P&W brand after eleven years of declines and made it the fastest growing brand in its category.

My team reversed a two year share decline on one of McHugh's most important brands and achieved the highest share gains in the brand's history.

I've built business teams from scratch, developed and introduced dozens of new products, expanded established brands, and identified, analyzed, and managed acquisitions.

If you have a business that needs help, perhaps we should talk. I look forward to your call.

Sincerely,

Martin H. Greenwall

Martin H. Greenwall

the broadcast letter on the previous page. It was written by a marketing executive. Did it work? Well, he must have done something right; his new position pays $25,000 more than the one he lost.

The LetteRes

Q.   *What do you do when you come across a position that you would love to apply for but your resume really doesn't pertain to?*

A.   *You write a LetteRes.*

Q.   *What do you do if your resume is so heavily weighted toward a particular industry that it inhibits your applying for a similar position in a different industry?*

A.   *You write a LetteRes.*

Dave Bartlett (the same Dave as in the previous story) had held the positions of Controller, Assistant General Manager, and Director of Finance/Operations all, except for a brief stint, with food manufacturers.

He wanted to remain in the Detroit area, but there were very few food companies in this locale large enough to accommodate someone with his credentials. Because he wanted to remain in the Detroit area the scope of his search was drastically limited.

It wasn't very long before he had exhausted his list of target companies. Now he began applying for Controller-type positions with other kinds of companies—with an overwhelming lack of success.

After lengthy discussions we came to the conclusion that Dave's resume was closing more doors than it was opening. He was sending it to the right people, the decision makers, but it just wasn't getting the job done.

Together, we decided that the resume was a strong one, but only when directed to food manufacturers. When Dave's resume reached an automotive manufacturer's desk, for example, it was quickly discarded.

Why? Because as soon as it approached the employer's desk he or she could smell the odor of food emanating from the envelope. The potential reader was quick to postulate:

"Bacon and beans? We don't produce bacon and beans. We produce barrels and bolts."

And *that* was the end of *that* story.

Also, the fact that Dave's experience was applicable to just about any field escaped the reader's imagination. Rarely do resume readers have the time or the inclination to try to ascertain the transferability of an applicant's work experience, skills, and education.

The answer? Obviously a new resume. But try as we did, we could not construct a resume that didn't smell like something from the oven. Thus was born what was called, for lack of a better descriptive word or term, a LetteRes.

Almost as soon as the LetteRes went out Dave's phone began to ring. His job search acquired new life. And, he landed an assistant-to-the-president position with a door manufacturer! Soon Dave's creative communique became known around the outplacement office as the "Magic Letter."

What Makes a LetteRes So Effective?

Its lack of specificity and its concentration on accomplishments.

I should acknowledge that the LetteRes is something I have really championed. It gets right to the writer's most saleable assets. This is what selling is all about. It also allows the writer to omit certain types of inappropriate information that might result in instant rejection.

For example, Dave's LetteRes never mentions a specific company or industry. In fact, it does not even indicate specifically what position he is seeking. Quite a neat trick. Don't you agree? This leaves the window of opportunity open for his being considered for the several positions he's listed.

Its conversational approach and its brevity.

Unlike the usual resume accompanied by a cover letter the LetteRes is but a single, easy-to-read, hard-hitting page. The reader reads it because it doesn't scare him or her away. He or she continues to read it because it contains the best, most powerful things the writer has done relating to the position in question. Because the writer's accomplishments are bulleted, this single-page document really packs a wallop.

It leaves the reader wanting more.

That "more" leads to a telephone call, which can lead to an interview.

Another job candidate in our outplacement program borrowed Dave's masterpiece to use as a model. No sooner had he mailed out about twenty-five or so of his own "Magic Letters" then he too had a hit.

The Magic Letter: The LetteRes

DAVID ROBERT BARTLETT
9 Huntington, Detroit, MI 48445
O: (313) 345-1234 H: (313) 322-6776

November 13, 1998

Mr. Charles Thomson
President/Chairman of the Board
Excell Quality Instruments
57687 Veryfine Avenue
Standout, MI 48907

Dear Mr. Thomson:

Due to operational relocation and consolidation, I am conducting a search for a senior level finance/operations position. My credentials include 20 years of progressive finance and general management experience, having held the positions of:

Director Finance—Operations Manager
General Manager—Controller

Most recently, I had bottom-line responsibility for a division with annual sales in excess of $60 million. My responsibilities included all financial, production, administrative, and warehouse and distribution activities. Accomplishments include:

- $300,000 per year savings achieved through revamping distribution network.
- $250,000 per year reduction in overhead expenses by reorganizing warehouse operations.
- 50% reduction in finished goods inventory levels through implementation of JIT system.

Reporting directly to the Corporate Vice President of Finance, my divisional responsibilities included the development of all systems and procedures, staffing, and implementation.

I am looking for an opportunity consistent with my career objectives—a top management position offering challenge, maximum accountability, and the prospect for professional growth. To discuss my qualifications in greater detail, I can be reached at the above numbers. I look forward to hearing from you.

Sincerely,

David Bartlett
David Bartlett

Proudly, he came to show me his LetteRes and to relate the reaction of an employer to this document. The employer began his conversation with this comment:

"Mr. Reese?"

"Yes."

"I'm sitting here reading this ... this ... well, I don't know what the heck you call it, but I have a few questions to ask you."

And *that* is how a LetteRes is supposed to work! Think you can do a job, but your resume doesn't indicate this? Seriously consider a LetteRes. If you dare to be brave, send a LetteRes in place of a resume. It stands a better chance of being read.

Recruiters

Writing to a recruiter is practically the same as writing to an employer. Naturally you want to strut your best stuff, but you also have to be careful. You don't want to give the recruiter a reason for rejecting you. The usual reason for rejection is the salary you might be making. All too often, it is too high or too low. My advice: don't state your salary needs. If he or she is interested, you'll receive a call.

If the number of people you supervised or the dollars you controlled are important to the level of the position you are seeking, by all means state them. However, once again, if these numbers may be too large or too small, don't give them, simply wait to be asked ... *after he or she is interested*. It's much better to communicate by voice, by phone or in person, than by mail. You have the opportunity to overcome rejections or explain circumstances. On the next page is just the body of a letter to a recruiter.

Thank-You Notes

Always, after every interview, send a thank-you note. Immediately upon returning home write the interviewer a note thanking him or her for the interview. Keep it short and sweet. Say you appreciated being granted time in a busy day.

A thank-you note is one of the easiest and nicest things you can do when looking for work. It can pay big dividends!

Broadcast Letter to Recruiters

November 3, 1997

Dear Ms. Crankston:

Several business acquaintances have mentioned the excellent reputation your firm has in conducting searches for marketing and sales people. Jack Scott, Director of Marketing at Dennison Corporation, suggested I contact you in the event you might be looking for a top-notch, very marketable candidate.

The track record I've enjoyed in both the automotive and consumer products businesses has been rather impressive. For example, I was:

- Promoted to National Sales Manager after only 2 years with my current employer. Here I directed the sales force in effecting an 8% increase in market share for all our products. We also enjoyed a 15% increase for 5 of our most well-known products.
- Instrumental in removing unnecessary "roadblocks" encountered by our salespeople in conducting time-consuming administrative tasks. This led to a 21% increase in profitability within 18 months.
- Recognized by senior management as one of the top 3 producers nationally in each company I have worked for.

At this stage of my career, I am very interested in evaluating opportunities with larger corporations offering greater responsibility and financial reward.

I am enthusiastic that my background will "fit" with a current search you might be conducting. I look forward to the chance to talk with you. I'll give you a call early next week to see how we might work to fulfill each other's needs.

Sincerely,

Robert Holland

Robert Holland

If you have ever interviewed people, you know how easy it is, after several candidates, to get them mixed up in your mind. Unless you take extensive notes it is difficult to remember who said what and which name belonged to which face.

You could be sitting there a day or two after the interviews, trying to put the pieces together, when in comes a thank-you note from one of the candidates. If this person is one of the favorites you are trying to sort out in your mind, it could be all it takes to turn the tide in his or her favor.

But a thank-you note is more than a way of showing your appreciation. To be truly effective it must also be a sales note, another opportunity to sell yourself. *Always remember, you are first and foremost a salesperson.* There is nothing you say or do in your job search that is not aimed at selling you.

Finally, a thank-you note can often create goodwill like an unexpected complimentary dessert after a good meal.

Thank-You Note Stationery/Cards

You can use your letterhead for your thank-you note. Or (and this is a personal preference), you can buy some nice preprinted thank-you note cards at your local stationery or gift shop. Don't buy something cutesy or flowery. Get something simple and elegant.

I buy my "tent style" cards at a local card shop. They are light gray, about 3″ × 5″ with "Thank You" embossed in silver script on the front.

Thank-you cards, especially the tent style, are much smaller than letterhead, so you don't have to worry about how you are ever going to find enough impressive things to say to fill a conventional page of stationery. Also, it is quite permissible to print or handwrite your "thank you" on a small formal card. The usual letter-size format calls for typing a response.

Another possibility? Monarch-size stationery. It's a little smaller than the usual size stationery, but quite a bit larger than a card. But remember, whatever you write, don't forget to sell yourself once again.

Here are two examples of sales-oriented thank-you notes written on the tent style cards I recommend using. The first note is in response to a possible job opening following an information interview. The second note is in response to a "regular" interview.

Thank-You Note—Example 1

October 23, 1999

Dear Ms. Lacy:

Thank you for the interview. I really appreciated your taking time to show me around your office building.

In reviewing my notes, I began thinking about your computerization project. There's no doubt in my mind that, given my C Basic and LAN expertise, I could hasten your implementation date by at least two to three months.

I will give you a call in a day or two to see if this is something we should discuss in greater depth.

Thank you once more for your courtesy.

Britt Anderson

Thank-You Note—Example 2

March 3, 1999

Dear Mr. Bright:

Just a quick note to thank you for your time and courtesy. I'm really excited about the possibility of becoming part of the Ajax team.

Incidentally, we seem to have strayed off the subject, but I do have refractory processes experience. In fact, I was selected to be part of a special task force that successfully introduced this innovative approach to Bixby's Oregon plant. Please remind me to fill you in on this the next time we meet.

Once again, thanks for your consideration and courtesy. I look forward to hearing from you in a week or so as promised.

Sincerely,

Joe Smith

Shot Down? Don't Give Up!

You probably wouldn't be surprised to learn nearly all job seekers fail to recontact the company upon being rejected. Before *you* join the ranks of the rejected don't give up so easily. Beating out your competition means doing those things your competitors fail to do. Of course, I'm not speaking of pie-in-the-sky things, but rather practical, down-to-earth activities that can sometimes produce surprising results. I'm also referring to activities that take up very little of your time; activities whose rewards far exceed the effort required to do them.

Think about giving the interviewer a call after you've been rejected. You may rest assured he or she won't be expecting one. There are a number of very good, logical reasons why you should employ this tactic. Get in the habit of calling after you've been rejected. It only takes a few minutes, but the results can be great.

When you call following an unsuccessful interview, guess whose name will be foremost in the decision maker's mind if:

- The person selected rejects the offer?
- The person selected doesn't work out?
- Another similar opening should suddenly surface?
- The employer receives a call from a business acquaintance or recruiter looking for someone with your type of experience?

Don't forget to ask the employer if he or she:

- Would be kind enough to suggest another company or person you should be contacting?
- Minds if you use his or her name?
- Would be willing to call ahead to pave your way?

Believe me, no matter what reason an employer has to unexpectedly fill an opening, the employer does all he or she can to avoid the bother associated with interviewing. You have got to be right there in the wings waiting, and he or she has to know that you are there. You must make every effort to be Johnny-on-the-Spot. You won't be Johnny-on-the-Spot if you don't try to place yourself in the spotlight.

Use the phone to make the initial contact. Then, follow up with a brief letter. Thank the employer for her time, courtesy, and valuable suggestions. Tell her:

- You hope she will keep you in mind for future openings.
- You hope she won't mind should you recontact her some-where "down the line."
- You will let her know how your search is going.
- You have contacted someone she suggested might help you.
- You have updated your resume and would appreciate her critique of it.

Finally, wait a couple of weeks and call back yet again "just in case" there might have been an unexpected development.

Guidelines for Writing Great Cover Letters

Follow these guidelines and you will greatly increase your ability to write successful cover letters. Refer to them—especially when you are writing your first dozen or so letters. Make them second nature. Even when you become good at it, look them over now and then to be certain you're maintaining high standards.

1. Keep it brief. Three to five short paragraphs. No more than one page. (Except perhaps for mini-proposals.)
2. Be concise. Use the twenty-to-ten rule. "Never say in twenty words what can be said in ten." Use as few multisyllable words as possible.
3. Write as you normally speak, but delete "that" whenever possible. See if "that" is really needed. Also strive to minimize the "you's." Be direct. Use plain English.
4. Be targeted. Direct your attention to the decision maker by name and title. Strive to meet the given or perceived job requirements. When you cannot meet a requirement, either ignore it or cite a suitable replacement.
5. No "weasel" words. Do not "think," "feel," "hope," or, "believe," that you can do the job. Be positive. Be assert-ive. Say, "I can . . . ," "I have . . . ," "I am . . . ," "I will . . ." Omit "however," "although," "but," "while," and "nevertheless."
6. Use correct grammar, spelling, and punctuation.

7. Minimize the "I's"—especially as paragraph lead-ins. Also, for appearance's sake, don't end a line with a lonely hanging letter such as an "I" or an "a."

8. Use an attractive format. Invite reading. Leave plenty of white space. Use bullets if possible, but avoid using so many that you "machine gun" the reader.

9. Use nice paper—off-white is suggested. Use the same letterhead for your cover letter that you do for your resume. Match your resume, cover letter, and envelope.

10. Use clean type. No erasures. No typeovers. No white-outs.

11. Follow the **W3SP** formula: Introductory Paragraph—**WHO** you are writing the letter to. Paragraph one—**WHY** you are writing. Paragraph two and possibly three—**SALES PITCH**. Paragraph four—state **WHAT** you would like to happen, or what the reader can expect to happen, next.

12. Sleep on it. If you can, put it away for a day or two, and then read it again. Try to be objective. Would *you* be motivated to act if *you* received this letter?

13. Read it aloud to a third party. Does he or she understand what you are saying? Are questions raised? Does it flow? Does it sound like you talking?

14. *Sell. Sell. Sell.* Use quantifiers if possible: dollars, numbers, and percentages. Tell what you can do to appreciably enhance the bottom line, to make life easier for your prospective boss. And, if possible, how soon you will make this contribution.

Summary

The cover letter introduces the resume. It is the appetizer before the entrée. Can your appetizer be devoured, pleasurably, within five to seven seconds? That's about how much time busy supervisors devote to such mail. This is especially true if they haven't advertised an opening. Will your letter make the reader look forward to the delicacies that await him or her?

Don't overlook using motivating letters to spur reluctant "hot" prospects into action. Just be careful to be diplomatic. No one likes to be backed into a corner and faced with an "or else" situation. If your letter projects such a tone, your goose is cooked; better not to have written.

Don't be afraid to create a letter to meet a particular need or situation. You just have to remember to keep it short, to the point, and to sell yourself. If you have given a position your best shot without obtaining results, isn't it better to try for it just one more time before giving up? What have you got to lose?

Chapter 4
How to Develop, Contact, and Pursue Job Leads

Y ou must use every resource at your command when prospecting for work—no matter how insignificant it might appear to be—no matter what the odds are against it paying off.

Never, ever, prejudge whether a particular person or company could lead you to the job you want. That's a good way to kill a possible lead even before it is given the chance to take seed. You need to talk to everyone, repeatedly, using every possible resource to lead you to these people.

Experts say that somewhere between 5 and 15 percent of all jobs are landed via employment agencies and recruiters combined. Does that mean that you should avoid what looks like a rather unproductive prospecting resource? Of course not. Your new job could be included in this small percentage, but it won't be unless you use this resource.

The great majority of job seekers confine their prospecting efforts to two resources: help-wanted advertising and employment agency recruiters. All the more reason to use every possible resource—your competition won't.

If you do not inquire about a job "opening," an employer cannot turn you away with the usual ". . . no openings" line. Therefore, your objective is to sit down and talk, face-to-face, with every possible prospective employer and network contact. Face-to-face meetings can and do lead to wonderful things, but you must get them to make them pay off.

Did you know that only 14 percent of all jobs are filled through help-wanted advertising? Employers do not advertise to fill positions if they can avoid it. They try to fill openings in-house first and then through people who recommend other people. It's cheaper, easier, and quicker than advertising. The moral of this story? Get the interviews, and the job openings will follow.

Networking

Networking involves contacting everyone you know *and don't know* to let them know that you're on the market. It involves asking people to contact everyone they know or to supply you with the names so that you can make the contact. When I say "everyone," I mean *everyone*. Employment experts insist that networking is the number one means of people finding work.

Get together with your: past supervisors, coworkers, wife, girlfriend, husband, aunt, father, best friends, long lost friends, local businesspeople . . . *everyone*, and complete the following network lists. Brainstorm; by yourself and with friends. Think of all the people you can under each category and add them to your network.

What you're looking for is a plethora of names. You can fill in the contact information later. Review these lists frequently. Keep trying to dredge up new names to add to the lists. As you come upon a new contact, add it to your list and contact that person before you forget him or her.

Don't think you don't know anyone that could help you. Think of people whom you admire, have done business with, and socialized with; people from all walks of life. Ask them for their help. When you contact them tell them, "I really need, and would greatly appreciate, any help you might be kind enough to give me."

When you're looking for work, the natural and first place to look is to companies and people in your industry. That's as it should be. But don't approach the most important aspect of your job search with tunnel vision. Just because you're looking for a job in plastics, doesn't mean someone like your friendly service station owner couldn't help you. Do you know all of his friends, neighbors, and relatives, business and social acquaintances? Do you know all of his customers? Do you know that one of his regular customers owns a plastics factory?

Now build your network. Build it long and strong. Never stop looking for new names to add to it. Remember, do not prejudge. Give people the chance to help you. You'll discover that most people love to help other people when asked politely.

RELATIVES

(close or distant—nearby or far away)

Name	Address	Telephone Number

FRIENDS

(old and new—high school—college—neighbors)

Name	Address	Telephone Number

_____

_____

_____

_____

_____

_____

_____

_____

_____

_____

_____

EDUCATION

(teachers—professors—principals—deans—coaches—counselors)

Name	Address	Telephone Number

WORK

(past/present—full/part time—coworkers/bosses/customers)

Name	Address	Telephone Number

SOCIAL CONTACTS

(religious—sports—clubs—organizations)

Name	Address	Telephone Number

_____

_____

_____

_____

_____

COMMUNITY CONTACTS

(politicians—retailers—professionals—personal business services)

Name	Address	Telephone Number

Using Your Network

Visit, call, or write to every person in your network. Select the ones most likely to be of assistance and work your way through all of the names. Actually visiting with each person is the best way to go; calling them on the phone is second best; and writing to them is a poor third.

When you contact them:

- Tell them . . . you're on the market and what kind of job you're interested in. If you have a second choice, mention this alternative position also.
- Ask them . . . if they know of any companies that might be interested in someone with your particular qualifications. Ask if they could suggest someone who could possibly help you out.
- Remind them . . . to keep you in mind and that you will be calling from time to time to see if they've come up with any new leads for you to pursue.
- Give them . . . a few copies of your resume "just in case." Insist they take them—no matter how slim they think their chances are of helping you out. If they place your resume on a desk or bureau top it will remind them you need their help and will be calling back to see what they might have come up with.

Don't Be Naive

Do you think for one moment that all your network contacts will actually distribute resumes for you? Hopefully, you're not that naive! Why then (you may ask), do I give them resumes, ask them to hand them out, and then inquire as to whether they need more? Here is a scenario for what you hope will take place.

The Networking Scenario

You give a long-lost friend three or four resumes—even though he insists he won't be able to use them. He goes home, empties his suit coat pocket, and pulls out your resumes, all folded up. He starts to throw them away but suffers sudden pangs of conscience and, instead, throws them on top of his dresser.

Every day when he gets dressed for work he "half-sees" your resumes on his dresser. Then, you call him back in a week or two to ask him if he needs some more.

> "Heck, no!" he exclaims. "I've still got the ones you insisted on giving me. I told you I didn't know anyone to give them to."

The trick is to keep calling him back every two weeks until he begins to complain to himself, "This guy is driving me crazy!"

Don't let this bother you. Exactly what you want to happen is happening. Between those resumes on his dresser and your calls, he'll be thinking about you; perhaps not in the kindest of terms, but you *will* be on his mind.

Then, your friend is out on the links, or in a barber's chair, and he hears about an opening for a . . . (whatever you're looking for) . . . Shazam! Suddenly, lights go on and bells begin to clang. Your unwanted resumes and your persistent nagging pay off. He remembers you. The rest will soon be happy history!

That's the way to work your network. It will only take a half hour a day to continually recontact a different segment of your network, but these thirty minutes a day can get you employed for a lifetime.

Networking and the Rule of Seven

Most job seekers have rather limited networks. And the unfortunate truth is that it is extremely difficult to sizably increase your network virtually overnight. What can you do to get the most out of the network at your disposal? The answer is to recognize and utilize the *Rule of Seven.*

The Rule of Seven has been kicking around in the sales world for years. It works, so why not adapt it to your needs? Here is what the rule states—it takes an average of seven contacts with a prospective buyer before you can expect to make a sale. If you have not made a sale after these seven contacts, move on to more productive ground.

Most job seekers feel rather uncomfortable calling a contact to ask if he or she knows of someone or some company that might need someone with their talents and experience. This uncomfortable feeling can develop into full-blown paralysis when the seeker is told he should contact each of his contacts more than once. And yet, as evidenced by the Rule of Seven: *it is imperative that each contact be contacted at least seven times.* The squeaky wheel gets the grease. Or, conversely, out of sight, out of mind.

But what can you say or do to maintain a high profile and not make a nuisance of yourself? Specifically, what seven things can you do to logically touch base with every one of your contacts once every two weeks? There is a fine line between being persistent and being obnoxious. Whatever you do, you had better not cross this line.

You say you can't think of seven valid, not-too-obvious, reasons? Not to worry. Here are twice as many, that's right, *fourteen*, for you to choose from.

1. Call to tell the contact you're on the market and would appreciate any leads or help he or she might be willing to provide. Try to arrange a get-together.
2. Call to ask if he would be willing to look at, and critique, your resume. Hand-carry it to him if possible. Leave extra copies "just in case."
3. Call to ask him out to lunch.
4. Call ". . . just to touch base"—to remind him that you need his help.
5. Call to see if he needs more resumes.
6. Call to update him on your search efforts.
7. Call to ask him to be a reference.
8. Call to ask if he's been contacted as your reference by someone.
9. Call for advice or suggestions.
10. Call to tell him the result of his advice or suggestion.
11. Call about something personal . . . a mutual friend or activity. Don't even mention the job search.
12. Call to ask what he might know about a certain person or company.
13. Send him a fax or a photocopy of a business article, announcement, development, etc., that might interest him.
14. Send him an updated resume or a supplement to your resume.

Still not enough ways to obey the "Rule of Seven?" OK, here is one more approach, no charge. . . .

15. Send him a thank-you note.

Using the Rule of Seven, your chances of a network contact producing a positive result are increased seven times.

It's better to recontact 25 network leads seven times than to contact 175 leads one time. It's not enough to let people know you're available and looking for a new job. If they don't remember you, what good does it do?

The Strength of Weak Ties

Talk to any experienced, skillful networkers and they will be quick to tell you about The Strength of Weak Ties. They probably won't have a name for this phenomenon, but they will certainly attest to its significance. You might think the people most likely to assist you in your job search are those you know the best. Wrong! You're more likely to receive rewarding support from those individuals three, four, or even five tiers down line from your network base.

Time and time again, job seekers report that people who didn't know them were the most helpful. Many more positions are found via down-line contacts than through primary resources. Why? I suspect it has something to do with those who know you best not being able to see the forest for the trees.

Effective networking demands you seek out and cultivate contact with people you don't even know. If you avoid reaching out to a friend of a friend for help, you severely hinder your chances of finding a great new position as quickly as possible.

The Library

Job prospecting and library research go hand in hand. Today's libraries have all types of manual and computerized information retrieval and storage systems. The modern library is truly a "nice place to visit," a place where you will feel right at home. The rapidly increasing number of Americans taking advantage of today's libraries attests to the validity of this statement. In fact, the library is also a favorite haunt for knowledgeable job seekers—and rightfully so.

There are libraries to meet just about any need. Larger universities often have several devoted to such disciplines as business, law, arts and sciences, and so on. Businesses, such as stockbrokers and attorneys, often have their own library facilities. Find them. Use them. You can develop more leads in a library in an hour than you can develop all week using every other means.

If you're looking for a specialized library in your vicinity or for a specific need, call or go to the nearest library. Ask if they have a publication called the *Directory of Special Libraries and Information Centers*. Here is a sample entry as might be found in this directory:

7700
Illinois Psychoanalysis Institute—Library (Med)
13320 Hayward Street   Phone: (401) 443-0678
Fairfield, IL 70889   Amanda Marie, Librarian

When using the library in your prospecting efforts you will soon discover that the types of reference books you need cannot be taken home. In fact, you may have to surrender your driver's license before being allowed access to certain of these books. The nature of these publications is such that they are in great demand and would also cost a pretty penny to replace should they vanish mysteriously. Plan on spending some time with these reference materials once you get there. Bring along a few pencils, a notebook, and a supply of change for the copy machine.

Librarians

Following are some of the resources at the library that you will find useful in job prospecting. Remember that there are many more references available for researching a specific company or industry. Think creatively. If you don't know where to find a certain type of reference book, or, for that matter, what reference books are available, ask the reference librarian. Librarians are almost always extremely helpful, knowledgeable, patient, and professional. They are paid to help you. The librarians I have encountered live for the challenge of locating hard-to-locate information.

Newspapers

Many libraries carry the Sunday editions of major newspapers from across the country. Usually they do not appear on the newspaper rack until two or three days following the date of publication. If you cannot find a library that carries Sunday editions, you might try to locate a busy newsstand or bookstore. The majority of help-wanted advertising is found in the Sunday paper. Remember, if you think you can do the job, go for it.

It's important you understand help-wanted advertising and how to utilize it effectively. So, get ready, here is all you'll ever need (or want) to know about help-wanted advertising.

Help-Wanted Advertising

Every job seeker is familiar with help-wanted advertising, it's far and away the most popular means of looking for work (although only 14 percent of all jobs are advertised). Because it's so popular, competition is fierce. You'll be lucky if the companies you respond to even drop you so much as a "thanks for applying" note. Sitting by the phone or watching for the mail carrier is an exercise in futility and a sure way to sink slowly into the depths of depression.

Does this mean to forget help-wanted ads as a means of securing a job? Absolutely not. Although competition is rugged, and the jobs for you are few and far between, remember the commandment: *when looking for work use every conceivable means.* Acquiring and responding to help-wanted advertising will comprise a small, integral part of your all-out campaign. It's imperative you understand how to most effectively use this resource. There are two types of help wanted ads: classified and display.

Classified Ads

These ads are found in the classified sections of newspapers and a few trade journals. The section they are found in is usually preceded by the heading *Employment* or by *Employment Opportunities*. In most publications they are listed in alphabetical order according to occupation or job title. It's relatively inexpensive to run a classified ad. Smaller, less well-heeled companies and organizations often use this medium.

Start-ups, nonprofit, and low-profit institutions and agencies, direct-sale, multilevel, and "no-experience-needed" type companies depend heavily upon classified advertising for hiring. Rarely will you find middle to upper-level positions advertised in the classifieds.

The following is a typical classified ad. You have undoubtedly seen some like it many times. How would you interpret it?

> Government Jobs $24–50,000. Vacancies must be filled immediately. 381-222-0000 Ext. B-525. Small fee.

An ad of this nature usually means someone has compiled a list of government job openings he or she would like you to buy. Whether these openings still exist or not is questionable. The location of many of these positions is just as questionable. If you have an extra $15 or $20 to shell out you could respond.

Here is another type of ad frequently found in the classified employment section:

High Earning Potential for motivated people seeking instant cash flow. 42 Park Plz, 2ⁿᵈ Flr, Ste

You can bet that this is a sales job, commission only—when you sell you make money; when you don't—you don't. Sell what? Just about anything—books, vacuum cleaners, or magazines are three of the more common items. Notice that they don't want you to call. When you visit them be prepared for the sales pitch of your lifetime.

When a number is given and you call, they will insist that you visit their office if you want to obtain details about the position advertised. Once again, they'll sit you down and give you a sales pitch. The next thing you know, you wind up out on the street peddling their wares. If a company won't tell you about a position over the telephone, chances are high that it's a waste of your time.

One more:

Die Maker or Tool Maker. Must be experienced on all tool room machines. Retirees or part-timers are invited to apply. Barkley Machines, Jenkins Rd, Rainbow City. 635-0011.

A small machine shop is looking for a jack-of-all-trades who will probably be expected to work on a part-time or as-needed basis.

Display Ads

Companies usually reserve display advertising for management, degree-required, or hard-to-fill positions. Newspapers generally carry these display ads (often called box ads because they are boxed in with some sort of typeset border) in one grouping preceding the classifieds. In trade journals, they are frequently located near the rear of the publication or mixed in amongst the articles and other advertising. Sometimes the company logo or special artwork is used along with eye-catching typesetting. This type of advertising falls into two basic categories.

Straightforward. In addition to a job description and job qualifications, contact information is given. If at all possible, you should try to come up with the name of the decision maker in your particular area and contact him or her instead.

PRODUCTION CONTROL

PLANNER/EXPEDITER

AEROSPACE MANUFACTURER HAS IMMEDIATE OPENING FOR A PLANNER/EXPEDITER:

B.S. degree in business administration or related studies. Knowledge of MRP II. Excellent communication skills. We offer a full range of benefits. For consideration send resume and references to: Wingz, Inc., 2300 Hutforth Dr, Fort Shilling, TX 75093, ATTN: HR, **EOE. /F/H/V**

Blind. Often called box ads because the contact information consists of a name or title and a box number. If it's a post office box, call the post office and ask what company placed the ad. Sometimes they will tell you. If it's a newspaper box ad and the position interests you, reply and move on. Maybe you'll get a response, maybe not. Frequently, this type of ad is placed by executive recruiters or employment agencies. In some states employment agencies are required by law to disclose themselves. Ads of this type also give the employer the opportunity to have a headhunter screen the responses before forwarding those that look the best to the employer.

PLANNING MANAGER

A large multihospital system in Southeastern Michigan seeks to fill a Planning Manager's position in its corporate Planning Department. This position requires an MS in Health Administration and at least five years' planning experience in a hospital or health care environment. Please send resume and salary history to: Detroit News/Free Press, Drawer C2232 P.O. Box 33, Detroit, MI 48441

Why would a company place a blind ad? For several reasons:

1. To eliminate an obligation to answer responses.
2. To test the water; is there that certain someone out there?
3. To maintain secrecy; maybe they don't want the current job holder to know they want to replace him.
4. Maybe their reputation is unenviable.

Responding to Help-Wanted Ads

- **Never reject yourself.** If you want a job and think you can do it, go for it. Companies will always shoot for the moon, and then be quite happy to hit a star.
- **Direct your inquiry specifically to the person in charge of your area.** Use the telephone. Second choice? The mail.
- **Never submit salary information.** If you ask for too little, your value as the right person for the position could be questioned. If you ask for too much, you could price yourself out of the running. Companies usually ask, but job seekers should never answer salary requests when responding to an ad.
- **Answer the ad immediately.** You will be one of the few job seekers not directing your reply to the person or department given in the ad. So why wait? Head your competition off at the pass. The person receiving your reply, the person in charge of your area, will not have many responses to read unless his or her name was given as the contact in the ad. Your competitor's replies will be piling up on someone's desk, while the boss reads yours. If you discover the ad some days after it appeared in the media, also reply immediately. He or she could be sitting there unhappy with the available choices when suddenly your bid arrives out of nowhere!

The Business Section

Large newspapers have a section of the paper reserved for business news. Depending upon the paper, some specific days are more heavily business news oriented than others. Included in the business section will be reports of promotions, resignations, hirings, and retirements. Also included will be news of mergers, acquisitions, expansions, and so forth. All of these areas involve change, personnel transactions. Change is almost always accompanied by job openings of one sort or another.

Keep your eye on the business section, as well as on the news in general, for announcements concerning product or service development. This type of information is useful as background material for phone calls, cover letters, and interviews—an excellent way of demonstrating to a prospective employer that you're alert and informed.

When reading business news articles try to become sensitized to problems companies are reported to be experiencing. It shows the interviewer you're aware of the company problem and care enough to want to do whatever you can to be part of the solution. And, once again, you're aware of what's going on in the industry.

Specific Reference Material

The Wall Street Journal

The *Journal* publishes a daily paper in regional editions. The help-wanted advertising you see in your edition of the *Journal* will largely concern companies in your region. Most of the ads are display ads. The Tuesday paper carries the largest number of ads. Most of the positions advertised are managerial or executive.

National Business Employment Weekly

This is a Sunday paper of help-wanted advertising gleaned from the regional daily editions of the *Wall Street Journal*. Again, the positions advertised usually call for higher education and in-depth experience. Therefore, the positions advertised are almost all managerial or executive. You can find the *National Business Employment Weekly* in pharmacies or bookstores that carry a large variety of newspapers. For subscription information call: (212) 808-6792.

Other Newspapers

There is contact information at the back of this book in Appendix D for major papers from some of the major cities in the United States. By no means is this a complete listing. Consult *Gale's Directory of Newspapers, Magazines, and Broadcast Media* for further listings. Many newspapers have websites as well. You can call or search on-line for their addresses.

Trade Journals

Trade journals are magazines devoted to specific industries, trades, or professions. They carry news of developments within these areas, and such news can be used as background information by prospectors. Trade journals are also another means of acquiring contact information for companies and people. A few trade journals will carry help-wanted advertising. You will also find position wanted ads placed by job seekers such as yourself. Very few jobs are landed via such ads. To locate trade journals in your area consult *The Serials Directory*, Ebsco Publishing, or *Ulrich's International Periodicals Directory*, R. R. Bowker, publisher.

The Yellow Pages

As you know, the *Yellow Pages* are alphabetized according to subject or service: Abrasive Blasting Machines, Abrasive Cutting, etc. Turn to subject(s) pertaining to your job search. Write down the names, addresses, and telephone numbers of the companies or businesses listed under this heading(s). Companies that "couldn't possibly be of any help" could develop into "hot" leads. Interviewing with a company you don't really care if you work for or not is wonderful practice for the "real thing."

Encyclopedia of Associations

Practically all businesses and professions have associations representing their members and their interests. The *Encyclopedia of Associations* lists these associations.

5344
Black Data Processing Associates (Information Processing) (DPA)
P.O. Box 7466
Philadelphia, PA 19101   Paul W. Foley, President

Founded: 1975. **Members:** 150. **Local Groups:** 8. Persons employed in the processing industry, including electronic data processing, electronic word processing, and data communications. Associate members are persons with an interest in information processing. Seeks to accumulate and share information processing knowledge and business expertise in order to increase the career and business potential of minorities in the information processing field. Conducts professional seminars, tutoring services and community introductions to data processing. **Publications:** *Data.* **Convention:** 1999 July, Troy, MI.

The Directory of Directories

The *Directory of Directories* is another invaluable reference book for job seekers. It lists hundreds of directories for all types of businesses, industries, and interests. Many of these directories are relatively inexpensive, while others are not quite as affordable. If you can't find what you're looking for, give your reference information to a librarian and he or she will check to see if they have the magazines or issues you need. Here is a sample listing:

2201
Accounting Firms & Practitioners
American Institute of Certified Public Accountants
1211 Avenue of the Americas
New York, NY 10036   Phone: (212) 575-6200

Covers: About 25,000 certified public accounting firms having one or more principals belonging to the institute, and accountants practicing independently who are members. **Entries Include:** Name, Address, Tel. #. **Arrangement:** Geographical. **Frequency:** Biennial, January of odd years. **Price:** $15.00, postpaid.

The Reader's Guide to Business Periodicals

This is an ongoing series of publications showing where to look in a wide assortment of business magazines for articles pertaining to a particular topic or topics. Look for this publication on microfiche and also as a database.

(Acquisitions and Mergers)
See also
Forest products industry—acquisitions and mergers.

Foster takes over Buton; Maxim Morphy stays independent. W.J. Bates. II Aviat Week Space Technol 117:234 0 4 '94 Behind the lines in the Buton war (attempted takeover by Foster/Burton of Maxim Morphy) Jesse Brine and K. Lipischak. II Fortune 106:156-8+0 18,94

Once you discover which magazines contain articles about your interest area, jot down the names and dates of the periodicals and head for the magazine racks. If you can't find what you're looking for, give your reference information to the librarian, and he or she will check to see if they have the magazines or issues you need.

Incidentally, if the library you're working in doesn't have what you need, they can usually tell you what library does have it. Sometimes they belong to interlibrary lending co-ops and can get the book you want from a co-op member. Of course, this does not pertain to reference books.

State Manufacturing Directories

Looking for a position in a manufacturing company? A manufacturing directory is a great place for leads. Manufacturing directories are published individually by state, with a few available for specific regions. They don't all use the same format, but generally they contain: the company name, its products, address, telephone number, and the names of the company executives or top-level managers.

Some directories will also provide information about the size of the facility, when it was established, the annual sales, and the number of male and female employees. Naturally, you want to use the latest edition when developing job leads. Some directories list each employer three ways:

1. Geographically
2. Alphabetically: by city and/or town within the state, by employer name
3. Products and Specialties

Sample Listing:

Acton–Pop. 24,000
Blakley Chemical Co.
Div, ASCO Chemical Co., Warren, OH
230 Brown Ave.
2991—Adhesives & Sealants
Branch Plants: Downey, CA; Palmer, MA
T. Noteman, Pres.; Dennis Riemer, V.P.; E. Roy, Pur. Agt.
Emp. 155 M., 50 F.; Est. 1945., Ph. 517-213-7678

Even though you may be referring to the latest edition of a directory, do not assume that the information is current. Call to verify the correct contact.

Dun & Bradstreet's Billion Dollar & Million Dollar Directories
Standard & Poor's Register of Corporations

These are three of the most widely used of all prospecting reference books. They contain contact information for thousands of top-ranked companies selected according to their net worth. These corporations cover a wide spectrum: industrial, utilities, banks, trusts, insurance, retailers, and wholesalers.

> **Northwest Smelting & Refining**
> 16 West Ave., Clayton, MS 77889
> Tel. (555) 234-9876
> **SIC 3341 5051**
> **Mnfr Smelters Refiners & Whl Watches**
> **Jewelry Supplying Precious Metals & Mercury**
> J. B. Paydos CH BD
> Noah Lambert PR

Newsletters

There is a newsletter published for practically every subject and topic. They are a good source of leads and background information. One place to look to see what is available is the *Oxbridge Directory of Newsletters*. This directory contains information for over 17,500 publications and is published by Oxbridge Communications, Inc.

Annual Reports

If a company is publicly held, look at its annual report. If your library doesn't carry these reports, simply contact the company or a stockbroker and ask to have one mailed to you. In addition to financial statements for the year, most reports name the top-level executives, what products and/or services they deal in, where their facilities are located, and their plans for the future. Just remember, you're reading the company line.

Other Prospecting Resources

State Employment Security Commissions

Often referred to as "The Unemployment Office," these commissions are state-run agencies and, therefore, the exact way they operate depends upon the dictates of each state. Some states offer job counseling and job search assistance through these offices. These agencies also serve as depositories for the Federal Job Bank, which contains openings for jobs that the federal government is connected with in some way. Ask your agency about this service. Find out what the security commission in your state can do to aid you in your job search. Look for your state agency under the state listing in the white pages of the phone book.

Example: In Michigan you would open the white pages to "Michigan, State of," and proceed to "Employment Security Administration."

Warning: All states do not refer to this agency as an Employment Security Administration. Look for other possible listings or call state government information.

Employment Agencies

Should you or shouldn't you? An employment agency sounds like an easy way to find a job, but you hear so many different stories about them, how they operate, how much they charge. Understand how they function and how to assess their legitimacy so you can use them, if possible, as another prospecting tool.

Employment agencies make the majority of their placements in the lower salary level positions, and typically place individuals who are seeking employment in the local geographical area. Most will actively try to place candidates with local employers. When they receive a job order, they will review their files for applicants or advertise in the local newspapers.

The fees are normally up to a maximum of 30 percent of your starting salary. Pay attention to who is paying the placement fee. Before you go on the interview, find out if:

1. Employer Pays the Fee—If the agency sends you on an interview and you are hired, the company that hired you pays the agency for sending you to it.
2. Job Seeker Pays the Fee—If the company hasn't agreed to pay the fee, and you are hired, you will end up paying the agency fee. Fortunately, this type of arrangement is becoming rare. Some states have even outlawed this practice.

Incidentally, it is recommended you not tell an employment agency counselor what companies you have already contacted about openings. He or she could send another one of their candidates to interview for those openings. If one should beat you out, you lose but the agency still wins. It still gets paid by the company.

How to Qualify Employment Agencies

- What is its placement success rate?
- Will they give you the names and telephone numbers for a few of their satisfied placements?
- Do they seem genuinely concerned with your interests? If not, ask the agency manager for a new counselor or go to another agency.
- Did they explain the contract to you point by point? Did you understand it? Were you completely satisfied with their explanations?

There are several kinds of employment agencies. *Specialized* agencies, for instance, include jobs for clerical workers, nurses, accountants, and so forth. *General* agencies represent job seekers in general. *Temporary* agencies obviously specialize in temporary help. This area has expanded greatly within the past few years, and now encompasses not only clerical and unskilled hourly positions, but in more recent years has grown to include technical and professional positions as well. Beyond utilizing temporary agencies to find employees to help out in an "overload" situation or to fill in for employees on vacation or sick leave, there are growing numbers of employers who like the idea of being able to try out an employee on a temporary basis. After a period of time, if this employee proves himself or herself capable, and he or she likes working at the company, the employer then invites the person to work directly for the company. This practice is often referred to as *temp to perm*.

Working for a temporary agency is not a bad way to get paid for discovering what various companies are like and how your job might vary from one day to another. In addition, temporary agencies can provide some real opportunities for parents who are re-entering the workforce after raising children.

Some employers are moving to *employee leasing*. This concept is not dissimilar to working for a temporary agency. You are hired by the employee leasing company, it pays you your wages and benefits, and you are assigned to work at one of its client companies. This relieves the client company of hiring, providing benefits, doing payrolls, filing employment related tax returns, and so forth.

Recruiters

Executive recruiters, search firms, headhunters—these are some of the better known and colorful names associated with placement firms that locate employees for employers. There are two basic types of recruiting firms, contingency and retained.

Contingency Recruiters

Contingency recruiters are hired to find candidates usually no lower than $30,000. They're hired to find candidates for professional, harder-to-find technical, middle management, and occasionally higher level management positions. They are paid only if they find the candidate who wins the position. Contingency firms sometimes have "exclusives," but most of the time they don't. Typically, they will send as many resumes of qualified candidates, and at times not-so-qualified candidates, as they can find for the position.

I have found that candidates who submit their resumes to, and try to arrange get-togethers with, contingency recruiters stand a fairly good chance of being considered. Although contingency firms are loathe to admit it, I have seen cases where the recruiter, upon finding a good prospect, will try to locate a corporate client whom he or she believes might be interested in this prospect. For this reason, I recommend that, if qualified, you contact contingency firms and continue to contact them on a discreet basis.

Retained Recruiters

This firm is hired by an employer to locate a specific type of individual for a specific type of job. Almost always, the individual they are looking for will fall in the $75,000 and up category. The recruiter will receive a fee of anywhere from 30 to 40 percent of the position's total compensation for the first year, plus out-of-pocket expenses—whether or not they find the winning candidate. For this reason, they are very particular as to whom they send to interview. After all, they won't receive many assignments unless they produce satisfactory results.

Many times, retained recruiters will work closely with the employer to help create or define the exact description for the position. They will work with the employer to define the position's duties and responsibilities, as well as requirements such as education, prior industry and job experience, and personal attributes. The retained recruiter has an exclusive assignment; his or her loyalty is to the company who hired him or her. In other words, he or she is not in business to get you a job.

Typically, the retained recruiter will personally interview a number of people for the position. If you are selected, the recruiter will prepare a report addressing your potential as a candidate for the position. This report, along with your resume, will be presented to the employer for consideration. Usually, the recruiter will present three to five candidates whom he determines appropriate.

Why do employers hire retained recruiters? Perhaps they are looking to replace a problem or unproductive executive, but they don't want to let this person go until they find his or her replacement. The employer may wish to keep the search confidential. In this case, the recruiter acts as the middleman. Should any advertising be done, it will be done by the recruiter, without revealing the employer's name. The employer may also be looking for a senior level management position or a hard to find management position. A retained recruiter will be focused on filling the employer's position.

Both employment agencies and recruiters will often want to have exclusive rights to represent you. They will tell you that you don't want the town papered with your resume. What will employers think? Poppycock. I look at finding a job like trying to sell a house. No more exclusives for me. I've been burnt a few times, having spent many anxious and futile hours waiting for my realtor to call. Now when I sell my house, I throw my hat in the ring and may the best man or woman win.

Some Recruiter Basics

It is natural that recruiters prefer to present employed rather than unemployed candidates to their client companies. But, if you're unemployed, don't let this deter you. Call to sell yourself. Send a resume and cover letter anyway. After all, losing your job in today's highly volatile job market is not an uncommon occurrence. If they like what they read, you will hear from them.

Bear in mind, a recruiter who fills ten or eleven positions a year is considered successful. Because client search requirements are often so stringent, the more candidates they know about, the better their chances of finding the right person. If you don't contact them, how will they know you're available and how great you are?

Also remember, a recruiter will usually submit two or three qualified candidates for employer consideration. This increases his or her chances for success. Don't expect to be the one and only candidate for a position. So, treat him or her with kid gloves. Being one of three candidates is better than not making the cut.

Contacting Recruiters

The bible for executive recruiters is called the *Directory of Executive Recruiters* and is published by Consultants News, Templeton Road, Fitzwilliam, NH 03477. Here you will find contact and specialty information for recruiters, contingency and retained, from across the country.

Besides falling into contingency and retained categories, most search firms devote their attention to a few specific occupations—engineering, finance, the food industry, etc. You must seek out and contact the appropriate agency for you.

Recruiters come and go like ships in the night. It's a tough business. How would you like to look for work for someone else every day of the week? Because they come and go with such rapidity it is essential that you use only the latest edition of this directory (or any directory for that matter).

As so often pointed out, a job search is a numbers game. Being such, you should seriously consider doing at least one mass mailing. Select those firms in your field and in your geographical target area and mail them a resume and cover letter. Never mention salary in your letter; it's too easy to be immediately disqualified.

Many firms have connections or offices in other cities. If you're from Boston and a recruiter there likes what he learns about you but doesn't have a job order, he will contact these other professional connections. Then, should you land one of these other positions, he will receive some type of compensation.

Don't be afraid to use mailing labels in your mass mailing. Recruiters are too busy to worry about how impersonal address labels may be. They are interested in top-notch people, not in mailing labels. You can purchase such labels from Consultants News. Don't waste valuable time typing up your own labels. You could and should be doing many more potentially rewarding things than typing mailing labels. One of these things is to recontact each of these agencies somewhere down the line, in two or three weeks.

After you have landed a position be certain to let all of your contacts know. In the case of recruiters, your employment will demonstrate your worth to them. You could very well be placed in their files for future consideration. Wouldn't this be an ego booster? It would be especially rewarding to be contacted out-of-the-blue if the job you are holding turned out to be less than you hoped it would be.

Chambers of Commerce

As you undoubtedly know, chambers of commerce can be found in local, regional, state, national, and international directories. They promote community good will and provide businesspeople with every opportunity to be successful at what they are doing.

Almost every chamber publishes a membership directory. If there is a particular town or city you would like to work in, contact the chamber in that community and ask to receive this directory. It should be a wonderful source for local job leads. The information published by most chambers of commerce also contains such local information as tax rates, educational opportunities, health and recreational facilities, etc.

Most chambers hold a monthly luncheon meeting. Try to attend one of these meetings. You'll be warmly welcomed. They're always looking for new members. While there, shake a few hands, pass out some resumes, and collect as many business cards as possible. If you have the time, try to set up some one-on-one get-togethers.

Places Rated Almanac

Published annually by Prentice-Hall, Inc., the *Places Rated Almanac* contains information for over 300 metropolitan areas, ranked and compared by: living costs, employment outlook, crime, health, transportation, education, arts, recreation, and climate.

"Career Counselors"

You've probably seen their ads in the Sunday paper help-wanted section: "Discover the Hidden Job Market," "The Best Jobs Are Never Advertised," and other similar headings. They call themselves "Career Counselors," but their counseling often consists of little more than helping you to write a resume and distributing a few hundred copies of it. For this, you can expect to pay anywhere from $2,500 and up.

Summary

There is absolutely no reason why you should ever run out of job leads. Not if you use *all* of the resources contained in this chapter.

Your most important source for job leads is networking. Use the methods and techniques described in this report to build your network. Don't expect your network to ever be complete. Continue to expand it and recontact it until you have landed a position—and even after! As you will discover more with each passing day, a strong network can be a powerful resource—not only for getting a job but also for conducting your business and domestic affairs. The network you create now can fruitfully reward and support you for the rest of your life.

The most important element in effective network usage is continued, repeated contacts. For this reason, there is probably nothing in this book as important as the Rule of Seven. Should you find yourself at a dead end, immediately check to see whether you have or have not obeyed this rule.

Very few openings ever make the newpaper. Companies take an easier, less costly, less time-consuming approach to filling openings. They look internally, officially or by word-of-mouth. Filling an opening in-house also makes the employees much happier than to see an outsider brought in.

Your mission is to expose and infiltrate this in-house network. What does this espionage pay? That depends solely upon how successful you are at accomplishing your mission. It could land you your "dream" job.

Chapter 5

How to Dial Your Way to a Great New Job

The beginning geometry student learns that the shortest distance between two points is a straight line. Those wishing to conduct the strongest possible job search must learn that the shortest distance between two jobs is also a line—a *telephone* line.

Of all the weapons in a job hunter's arsenal, none is more powerful or less used than the telephone. Even job seekers who understand and acknowledge the truth of this statement would rather lick a stamp than dial a number. In fact, that's precisely what nearly all of them do . . . and that's good for you. The telephone provides an amazingly quick way for you to outmaneuver your competition and truly leave them in the dust.

Use the knowledge you are about to learn to overcome your fear of phone rejection. Force yourself to bite the bullet. Pick up the phone and do it! Practice what you learn here daily. Learn and profit from your mistakes. You'll soon be a power user. As Franklin D. Roosevelt said, "The only thing we have to fear is fear itself."

You are undoubtedly afraid that you will make an important call and blow it. This is probably true, especially in the beginning. So, start by calling employers you're not even sure you would want to work for. These calls will provide a wonderful opportunity for you to practice your interviewing techniques. I call this spring training. Even the all-stars go through this ritual. By practicing your technique on jobs you have no feeling for, you're ready to step up to the plate when your dream job comes up.

Where to Begin

As you should know by now, in nearly all instances, the manager of a particular function or department makes his or her own hiring decisions. Therefore, the place to begin isn't where your competition does. Don't mail your resume to another person or department unless you have absolutely no other recourse. Begin by trying to find out who your prospective boss would be in the company you are interested in.

There are several ways of obtaining this vital information. One way is to ask around or look in a directory to see if the person you need to contact is listed. (See Chapter 4, "How to Develop, Contact, and Pursue Job Leads.") Unless you are going for a middle manager position or higher, this approach will probably yield very little except the company's address and telephone number. But that's good! This is information you need to take the next approach.

The Mailing List Routine

Look up, or obtain from the information operator, the phone number of the target company. Dial this number. When someone answers say:

> **You:** *I'm updating my mailing list. Is your street address still*
> *___(reciting the address)___?*

Sounds off the wall, doesn't it? But companies call other companies all the time to update their mailing lists. The receptionist is used to this question. In almost every instance she'll respond without hesitation.

> **Receptionist:** *That's correct.*
> **You:** *And your zip code is still ___(whatever)___?*

Receptionist: *That's right.*

You: *Who is in charge of ___(your area of interest)___?*

Notice how smoothly you segued from innocuous, nonthreatening, questions into the important one? This transition and the information it generates is why this mailing list routine is so effective.

When you ask, "Who is in charge?" you can expect to encounter a few rather routine responses. Let's take the easiest first:

Response #1

You: *Who is in charge of ___(your particular area)___?*

Receptionist: *That would be ___(his or her name)___.*

You: *Would you spell that for me, please?*

Receptionist: *That's spelled ___(spells the name)___.*

You: *Is that Dr./Mr./Mrs./Miss/Ms. ___(name)___?*

Receptionist: *(She responds accordingly.)*

You: *And ___(his or her)___ correct title is?*

Receptionist: *(She gives correct title.)*

Note: As you are given this information, you record it on a *lead sheet*. This record-keeping procedure is included in Chapter 7 and Appendix C.

Response #2

You: *I'm updating my mailing list. Is your street address still ___(whatever)___?*

Receptionist: *That's correct.*

You: *And your zip code is still ___(whatever)___?*

Receptionist: *That's right.*

You: *Who is in charge of ___(your particular area)___?*

Receptionist: *I'm sorry. We don't seem to have a department by that name.*

You: *Perhaps you'll find it under ___(different name)___. Or under ___(another different name)___.*

Maybe she will. Maybe she won't. But at least you tried.

Response #3

You: *Who is in charge of ___(your particular area)___?*

Receptionist: *Who am I speaking with, please?*

You: *This is ___(your name)___. That's spelled _____.*

Receptionist: *Is there something I could help you with?*

You: *Yes, I'm sending my resume out and would like a name to direct it to, please.*

What if you should end up being "shot down"? So what? Check your pulse. You'll discover you are still very much alive. You might feel a little rejected, but life will go on!

Let's suppose you can't come up with a specific name to contact in your area of interest. Then you can always call Human Resources and, using this very same routine, try to arrange an interview with the Human Resources Manager.

Remember to ask for the correct spelling of the person's name, his or her correct job title, and whether that's Dr., Mr., Mrs., Miss, or Ms. If you are recording this information on a Lead Sheet you won't have to worry about forgetting to ask for all of this vital information, you'll just fill in the blanks.

That's it. That's all there is to it. That's the way to try to find out who you should be contacting, the decision maker in your area, within a company. This is the stuff of which successful job searches are made.

One last tip about using the mailing list approach. Use the KISS formula: "Keep It Short and Simple." Don't waste time with small talk. Don't even bother introducing yourself. Most receptionists are too busy for introductions.

The information needed to develop a job lead can be as easy as this to obtain. However, it is at this point that most job seekers face a dilemma.

Getting the Interview by Phone

What do you do now that you have the contact information? Do you:

A. *Continue the conversation with the receptionist and ask if you could please speak to Mr. Andersen?*

or . . .

B. *Quickly hang up. Then, mail your resume to this contact?*

It doesn't take a genius to know the right answer to this question. But it does take courage to actually ask to talk to the individual. Before you waver like most other job hunters when they find themselves in this dilemma, let there be no mistake . . . if you expect to maximize your job seeking efforts, if you want to conduct the strongest, most effective search possible . . . *you must talk directly to the person in charge of your area.*

The purpose of the call is to get the interview. The purpose of the interview is to get the job. And so, to succeed in landing a job as quickly as possible, you cannot quit now! You must ask to speak to the person in charge, the boss. And, when you do speak with this individual, you must press on for the interview.

You:	*Could I speak with Mr. Andersen, please?*
Receptionist:	*Just a moment, please.*
The Boss:	*This is ___(gives his or her name)___.*

Let's break the ensuing conversation with the boss into three separate blocks of dialogue or phases: *The Introduction, The Sell,* and *The Close.* Although these phases are separate in nature, you'll proceed from one to the next without stopping.

If the following looks like a lot to do, it's because the various options you can sometimes use are presented one after the other. Remember, you don't want to let the listener interrupt you because he might then assume control of the conversation, leading you away from your single-minded goal of obtaining an interview. It's easier to get "on a roll" if you don't let the listener cut you off at the pass.

Phase One—The Introduction

A. Introduce yourself.

> **You:** *Mr. Andersen, this is ___(your name)___. That's spelled ___(spell it)___, from ___(company)___.*

Why bother to spell your name? First of all, you want the listener to remember it and use it. Secondly, if the listener is deeply involved in something when you call it helps to gain his or her attention. Then, if at all possible . . .

B. Drop a name.

Drop the name of: a personal friend, a business or social acquaintance, an organization, a company, your employer, or anyone you can come up with whom the listener might know.

> **You:** *My best friend, Ed Matthews, retired from Coxson Company (the employer you are calling) recently, and he suggested I give you a call.*

or . . .

You:	*I had a meeting the other day with Jean Brown at Big Time, Inc. and she suggested that I give you a call.*

or . . .

You:	*I've been with Martin Accounting for the past five years, but I'm really interested in career opportunities with Coxson Manu-facturing.*

C. Say something nice.

If you can, say something nice about the company, the person you are talking to, or the company's product or service. Be certain that what you say is genuine. Whatever you choose to say, it doesn't have to be earth-shattering. It might be as simple as:

You:	*I've driven past your facility on the way to work every week for the last four years. I've always been impressed by how great your plant and grounds look. It's obvious that Coxson takes great pride in its image. Yours looks like the kind of company I would like to contribute to.*

or . . .

You:	*I've been using and recommending your products for years. I'm very interested in becoming an integral part of a quality company like Coxson.*

or . . .

You:	*I just read an article about your company in [a recent manufac-turing] magazine. Coxson appears to be the kind of employer I would like to devote my career to.*

Try to say something nice. But, if you can't say something nice, *don't* make something up just to satisfy this objective. Don't try to appear as something that you are not.

Spring Training

Practice your "pitch" until you are comfortable with it. Try it on companies you have no aspirations about joining. As I mentioned earlier, I call this "spring training," and even all-stars attend spring training. After you've practiced and you're getting good at it, start dialing your target companies.

Please do not skip over this phase of this exercise. Study it closely. Get a friend or relative and do some role-playing. Practice and be prepared.

Phase Two—The Sell

Present your sales pitch.

Get ready to give it your best shot. Keep it brief (around 15 to 30 seconds). Tell the listener a reason why he or she should want to get together with you—right away. Use a SOAR statement (See Chapter 1, "How to Leave the Competition in the Dust."), or an accomplishment statement that stresses, if at all possible, a profit-oriented result.

You: *Having worked for one of your competitors, I'm very familiar with your product. I'm confident I could make a valuable contribution to your team. Perhaps my greatest contribution could be in developing new accounts. As an account executive with Mercury Motors, I developed 20 new accounts within an eight-month period generating an additional 1.2 million dollars in sales.*

or ...

You: *I have a doctoral degree in environmental studies from Harvard University. My particular expertise lies in the area of development and implementation of environmental control equipment and machinery. I have had several research articles published in* The Environmental Journal. *One of these articles, "Waste Removal Management Systems for the Twenty-First Century," won the 1994 Journal's prize for Environmental Achievement.*

Phase Three—The Close

Do not stop—GO! Go for the Get-Together. Tell the listener what you want to take place as a result of the conversation.

You: *I'd like to stop by briefly to introduce myself and give you my resume. Which day would be better for you? Wednesday or Thursday?*

Did you catch that last statement? You probably know that this is called the "choice" close, a standard close used by sales people. If the company is located nearby, use it. It gives the listener a choice, rather than an opportunity to respond with an automatic "no." If the listener can dispose of you with a simple "no," you may rest assured, nine times out of ten, he or she will try to do so.

Don't ask questions that can be answered with a "no." Whenever you fail to obtain the interview ask yourself immediately "Did I get a 'no' answer?" If you did, you invited the answer by the way you phrased the question. Practice phrasing things in such a way that it is virtually impossible for the employer to reject you with a quick "no." Be nice. Give the listener a choice: "Which day might be best for you? Monday or Tuesday, Wednesday or Thursday, Thursday or Friday?" Should you receive a "no" answer in a telephone conversation with an employer, recognize immediately that you have violated this commandment.

Let's review the three phases your dialogue with your prospective boss should have taken.

"Desperation Breeds Success"

The middle-aged gentleman exuded class and charm. His manner of speaking, his appearance, his courtly bearing—all bespoke his executive capabilities. He was unemployed, but the choice was his own. He no longer could tolerate the rather unethical way that his institution operated, so he resigned. Now, nearly four months later, he was getting restless. The time had come, he decided, to reenter the business world. However, there was a slight problem. His job search was going nowhere. When he registered for job search counseling he was obviously becoming anxious about his future.

> *"Tell me," I asked, "how have you been going about looking for work?"*
> *"Here's my resume," the executive answered. "I must have mailed out a hundred of them."*
> *"OK. And what about the telephone?"*
> *"Telephone? What about the telephone?"*
> *"Have you been using the telephone?"*
> *"No."*
> *"Why not?" I asked.*
> *"I prefer not to," the distinguished job seeker responded haughtily.*

For the next two months the executive and I were in a veritable stand-off. I continually implored him to start using the telephone in his search, but he adamantly refused to follow my advice.

The problem the executive was having was precisely the same problem faced by less distinguished and less credentialed job seekers. He was afraid of rejection. But, at his level, the problem was worse because he was so accustomed to being in control of all kinds of situations.

After a few more weeks of waiting in vain for the postal carrier to arrive bearing the news he sought, the executive's resistance crumbled. Swallowing his pride and his fear, he began learning and practicing his phone technique. Much to his amazement and personal gratification, the results of his efforts quickly bore fruit.

He soon became the consummate telephone prospector. He obtained interviews in New York, Chicago, and Houston—all at company expense—and *he* was the one that initiated each contact, *by phone*. The last time I saw him was three months after he landed a position. Much to his surprise and delight, companies were still calling him to see if he was still looking for a job because they now had an opening that would fit him perfectly.

1. Phase One—Introduction: Introduce yourself. Spell your name. Try to "drop" a name. Say something nice.
2. Phase Two—Sell: Launch directly into Phase Two from Phase One. Make your pitch. Keep it brief.
3. Phase Three—Close: Launch directly into Phase Three from Phase Two. Don't ask "no" questions. Get the get-together.

Expect Problems

It would be incredibly naive to think that you won't run into problems now and again using this approach. Fortunately, you can prepare for the two most common ones.

Problem #1

Boss: *I'm sorry. We're not hiring at this time.*

Solution

You: *I understand. What I would really like to do is to meet you and give you my resume. It could save you considerable time and money when a position does open up. I could stop by next Wednesday or Thursday. Which is better for you?*

Problem #2

Boss: *I'm sorry, we don't have an opening in your area.*

Solution

You: *Truthfully, I would have been surprised if you did have an opening. But, I'd still like to stop by briefly to introduce myself and give* *you my resume. You never know when you might need to add to or replace a member of your team. I would like you to know that I'm standing in the wings, ready and qualified. What time might be best for us to meet for a minute or two?*

It's amazing the number of "not hiring" and "no opening" companies that suddenly find an opening for you when someone in a position of authority takes a liking to you. It's also amazing how an employer can take an initial liking to you just by talking with you on the phone. You must make every effort, given the right circumstances, to sit down and meet the employer face-to-face.

Most job seekers seem to feel that to call the prospective boss is to risk angering him. Yes, sometimes it does upset him. But it's just as likely to demand his respect. Just bear in mind, when you do get through to the boss you had better have something worthwhile to say. Always give at least two or three reasons why he should want to meet with you. Think profit!

The Secretary

You're no doubt thinking, you've covered receptionists and bosses, but what about the secretary? What happens when a secretary takes my call? Everybody knows that the secretary can control the drawbridge to the castle.

No matter how skilled you may become contacting and talking with employers, a few roadblocks will be thrown in your way every once in a while. Usually it's the same two or three, and they invariably involve the secretary. They are really no big deal, if you are prepared for them.

Follow the "Make a Friend" rule when talking to a secretary; *treat her with respect and make her your friend.* Don't try to bulldoze her, end-run her, deceive her, or "honey" her to death.

Let's role-play a little more. Here is the first of three situations commonly encountered with secretaries.

Situation #1

Secretary: *Mr. Andersen's office. Can I help you?*

You: *This is _____. That's spelled _____, from Carter Engineering. Mr. Andersen, please.*

Sometimes the call will be put through without your being asked another question. However, more often than not, she will be unable to connect you.

Secretary: *Just a moment, please.*
(a pause)

She might disappear for a few seconds before returning to say:

Secretary: *I'm sorry _____ I can't seem to locate him. Could I have him give you a call?*

No. You do *not* want him to call you. He could very well catch you at a bad time. You want to be psychologically prepared when you speak with him. You want to be ready to use the sales approach you have worked on. Or he might have to call back several times only to discover you're looking for a job. When he learns he has spent valuable time repeatedly calling someone looking for a job you'll not be one of his favorite people. But, you risk alienating his secretary if you reply to her question with an abrupt "no." What can you do?

Here is an excellent way to respond to this common question. This response works so well it's one of the few job search techniques you should memorize word for word:

You: *Thank you. I appreciate that. Who am I speaking with, please?*
Secretary: *This is Mrs. Murphy, his secretary.*
You: *Mrs. Murphy, I'm going to be away from my desk most of the day. He probably wouldn't be able to get me if he called. Perhaps you'd be kind enough to suggest a good time for me to call back?*

And you know what? In almost every instance she will!

Secretary: *You might give him a try first thing tomorrow morning.*
You: *Thanks, Mrs. Murphy. I appreciate your help. I'll give him a call at that time. Bye.*

Analyze this approach. Why does it work so well?

It works because you obeyed the "Make a Friend" rule for dealing with secretaries. You treated her politely, with respect. Review how many polite expressions you used without being obvious or obnoxious. You took the first steps in making her your friend. You treated her politely and you addressed her by name. Notice how skillfully you were able to call her by name without being transparent or obviously phony.

She has suggested a time to call back. What do you say when you call at that time?

Secretary: *Mr. Andersen's office. Can I help you?*
You: *Mrs. Murphy? This is _____. I talked with you on*
                _____. You suggested that I give Mr. Andersen a call at this time.

Notice that you opened the contact by calling her by name. Then you reminded her that it was she who told you to call back at this time, subtly shifting the responsibility for your being able or unable to talk with the boss onto her shoulders.

In all probability, he'll still be unavailable when you call back as suggested. Bosses are busy people. She might very well have to suggest another time or times for you to call back.

The more times you call unsuccessfully, the better you get to know one another and the worse she feels about your being unable to achieve your goal.

She may even go out of her way to help you.

Secretary: *(Calling you by name.) I feel terrible about your having to call*
                back so many times. If you promise not to tell him I told you, why
                don't you try calling back before eight thirty in the morning? I'm
                not in that early, but Mr. Andersen is. If you let the phone ring he'll
                most likely answer it. But don't tell him I told you that!

Sometimes a secretary is under strict orders to screen all calls. If this is so, she will attempt to qualify your call so that she handles it correctly:

Situation #2

Secretary: *Mr. Andersen's office.*
You: *This is _____ from _____. That's spelled _____. Mr.*
                Andersen, please.
Secretary: *May I tell him what this call is about?*
You: *Certainly. (Politely.) Who am I speaking with, please? (The begin-*
                ning of a possible friendship.)
Secretary: *This is Mrs. Murphy, Mr. Andersen's secretary.*
You: *Thank you, Mrs. Murphy. I'm calling to arrange a get-together*
                with Mr. Andersen.

Notice that you did not say you were looking for a job or trying to arrange an interview. Refrain from using expressions connoting job seeking. Using search related expressions is a great way to invite a quick phone transfer to Personnel. Sure you are calling to get an interview, but just don't call it that. Use "get-together" instead.

Perhaps you will be connected. It is just as likely however, that she will say:

Situation #3

Secretary: *May I tell him (or he would like to know) what this get-together is about?*

You've reached the court of last resort. You're obligated to tell her you're looking for a job. Unless of course, you come up with a better *truthful* response. But, you still don't say you're "looking for a job." Another response could be:

You: *I'm calling to talk with Mr. Andersen about career opportunities with Coxson Manufacturing. (If you can, add a line such as . . . I'm a close friend of a former business associate of Mr. Andersen.)*

The secretary may put you through now, but there's a good chance she will still try to screen your call.

Secretary: *Mr. Andersen isn't available. Could I help you with something?*
You: *I would really like to meet Mr. Andersen to give him my resume. Can you tell me a good time to stop by?*

If you can't meet the boss, meeting the secretary and giving her your resume, especially after you have treated her with politeness and respect, is the next best thing.

Voice Mail

Thanks to voice mail, it will sometimes seem impossible to get through to a real live person, let alone your contact. If you keep getting your contact's voice mail, try to get back to the secretary or switchboard operator. Most systems have an option available for this. The secretary or operator can often locate your contact or let you know a good time to call back. If at all possible, be sure to work through him or her rather than leave a message on voice mail.

What if you absolutely have to leave a voice mail message? Unless it's a referral call and you're attempting to develop a network lead, don't say you're looking for a job, or even worse, a job opening. Also, it's not a good idea to ask your contact to call you back. Let him or her know when you'll be calling again so he or she is expecting your call.

When you compose the message, try to think of some information about you that your contact might be interested in. You could say something like this:

> *"Ms. Smith. This is Sandra Jones. Jones is spelled just as it sounds, J-o-n-e-s. I've been with Ace Utility Company for the last ten years as an Industrial Engineer. I'm sure you're familiar with the refractory lighting process a friend and I developed. As you know, use of this process propelled my employer to the forefront of this industry. I now have some ideas for improving it that you should find interesting. I'm away from my desk much of the time so I'll try to reach you again tomorrow morning. Thank you."*

The key to receiving a pleasant reception lies in saying something the employer might have an interest in. If it's a vital interest, all the better. For this reason, you should try to incorporate a SOAR statement (see Chapter 1, "How to Leave the Competition in the Dust") within your message. Then, even if the listener realizes you're looking for a job, he or she still might be interested in finding out more about what you could possibly do for him or her. Here is a goal to shoot for in composing messages for voice mail; leave the listener wanting more. Arouse his or her curiosity. You must sound like you're the best thing since the invention of sliced bread.

Using a referral's name is also an effective way to gain your contact's interest. You could say:

> *"Ms. Smith. This is Sandra Jones. Jones is spelled just as it sounds, J-o-n-e-s. I've been with Ace Utility Company for the last ten years as an Industrial Engineer. Your golf buddy, Tammy Brookings, suggested I give you a call. She thought you might be interested in discussing some of the things I have been doing in the line of light refracturization. I'm going to be in and out all day today so don't bother to call me back. I'll give you a call first thing in the morning."*

Hopefully, the next time you call, your contact will be more likely to take the call after hearing your message. If you don't have the advantage of some information and/or a name the employer would be interested in, and you absolutely can't get through to him or her, it can't hurt just to leave a straightforward message. You could say something like this:

> *"Ms. Smith. This is Sandra Jones. Jones is spelled just as it sounds, J-o-n-e-s. I have 10 years' experience as an industrial engineer in the utility business. I would really appreciate the chance to meet with you and discuss my resume. I'll try to reach you again tomorrow morning. Thanks for your time.*

You never know, Ms. Smith may be looking for a new industrial engineer and decide to take your call.

Every time you try to reach your contact, remember to *treat the secretary with respect and make a friend.* When you get to know the secretary via the phone she also gets to know a little about you. If you've treated her nicely, she'll be impressed by the little she knows about you. In telling the boss that you called, she might add a comment or two about how nice you sounded, or how polite you were, or how anxious you seemed to be to talk with him or her. Now you are more than a recorded voice. You are a voice with a personality. And that doesn't hurt your reception at all. She might even suggest a good time for you to call back in order to talk directly with her boss.

There you have it. How to contact an employer, the people and situations you can expect to encounter, and how to handle them. Obviously, it is impossible to prepare you for every conceivable type of situation. But armed with the knowledge garnered from the examples presented here you should be prepared for just about anything.

The first seven or eight times you call to talk with employers, you'll feel like what you have to say is taking an hour per call. To minimize this feeling prepare a little script and refer to it. Keep plugging away. Through persistence and practice you will get better at it. Others, far less capable and talented than you, today occupy positions they enjoy because they refused to be denied. The shortest distance between two jobs? It is indeed the telephone line.

Beating the Odds

How many of your fellow job hunters do you think will try to contact their prospective bosses? How many will actually have his or her name, its correct spelling, and his or her correct title? Finally, and most importantly, how many will actually try to talk to this individual on the phone?

When you call and talk with the boss he has got to be impressed by your initiative, your ability to ferret him out, your ability to get through to him, and your ability to state your case. This has to be true even if you couldn't talk to him in person, but did mail or drop your resume off to him. Put yourself in his shoes. Is this the type of employee that you would like to have on your team? You bet it is.

Tips for Effective Telephone Prospecting

- Make secretaries your friends.
- Keep it brief.
- Sell.
- Don't ask "no" questions.
- Close with "Which would be better for you?"

Now we are going to take a look at using the telephone to pursue and develop that all important database . . . your network.

Contacting Network Leads by Phone

We all feel a little uneasy when it comes to calling people we have never met for help in our job search. Nonetheless, if you really want to maximize your chances for success this is an activity that must be done and done right.

When I say "done right," I mean that you must come away from each network cold call with as much pertinent information as possible. Leads are too hard to come by to waste them by not maximizing any assistance they might offer you. Get all you can from them. To do this, you must be aware of the types of information you need to fuel your search.

The Cold Call

The first thing to do, just as in the earlier telephoning examples, is to:

Tell the listener your name, spell it, and then your referral's name:

> *"Bob. My name is Don Lussier. That's spelled L-u-s-s-i-e-r. Gerry Tuttle suggested that I give you a call."*

Ask if he has time to speak with you:

"Is now a good time to talk?"

or . . .

"Do you have a minute?"

If he isn't able to speak with you just now, ask for a good time to call back. If he does have the time to speak with you:

Proceed by repeating your name:

"Thank you. As I said, my name is Don Lussier, L-u-s-s-i-e-r. I'm in the middle of an intensive job search and Gerry suggested you might be able to help me."

Give your job title or what type of job you're interested in (and if appropriate) what company you're from:

"I've been a copywriter with Martin Advertising in Santa Ana for the last six years."

or . . .

"I've been in the advertising game for the past six years. I'm attempting to transfer my experience into a new arena."

Give a brief synopsis of your background.

Highlight your most impressive achievement(s). Keep it brief, no more than 45 seconds.

"I've written newspaper and magazine advertising copy as well as copy for radio and TV. I don't know if you're familiar with the Cassidy Award. It's an award given by the California Radio/TV Guild for the most original and effective commercial. They present two awards each year; one for radio and another for television. I conceived of and wrote the copy for the commercial that won the 1995 radio award. Perhaps you may have heard it. It's the one for Interstate Movers. It features a little old lady, an enormous Russian wolfhound, and a pink and yellow moving van."

Ask for names of companies that might employ someone with your background and experience:

"Bob, I'm hoping you might be able to suggest a company or two that might be able to use someone with my background and experience."

Ask for names of people who might be able to help you:

"Would you happen to know anyone in particular that might be able to help me out?"

Get the spelling:

"How do you spell that?"

Get the company name:

"Who is she with?"

Get the title:

"What is her title?"

Get permission to use the contact's name:

"Might I use your name when I call her?"

Thank him for his help and/or time.

Ask if he minds if you keep in contact with him. Tell him you'll send him a resume. Perhaps he might run across something now that he knows who you are and what you're looking for.

You'll note that I don't recommend asking people if they know of an appropriate job opening. The odds of anyone knowing of a company with an opening you could fill are slim to none. (Of course, if the person with whom you are speaking works in your industry or field these odds are somewhat improved.) If they do know about an appropriate opening they will volunteer this information. If you ask, and they don't know of such an opening you'll receive a curt "no" for an answer. The ensuing conversation is usually brief and downhill.

It's difficult to converse with an individual who has just told you that he or she can't help you. It's the same as calling an employer and asking if he has a job opening. The answer is almost always "no." He or she probably *doesn't* have a job opening, and it's real convenient to say "no" and cut the conversation short. If you ask a "no" question you will receive a "no" answer.

Summary

There are hundreds of books and manuals and countless magazine and newspaper articles concerning job search. The significant difference between all of these books and articles and this book is contained in the chapter you have just concluded; in particular, how to use the telephone as a prospecting tool. You will have to search long and hard, and probably to no avail, to find another job search book that contains this specific information—information that is practical and works.

These techniques were developed and tested "in the field." They were studied, altered, and perfected through the counseling and observation of countless job seekers who actually practiced them. As you will soon discover, people looking for work don't have time to waste on brilliant but impractical suggestions. Therefore, it is possible to state unequivocally, this information works—if you give it a chance to—if you persevere and keep practicing. And, if you want a job badly enough you will.

Chapter 6
How to Amaze and Delight Interviewers

All of the exercises you've labored over, all of the information you have assimilated, *everything,* has prepared you for the moment of truth—the interview. Discovering or better defining: who you are, what you want, what you have to sell, who might be interested in buying, how to package yourself—these things had to be addressed to prepare you to interview with self-confidence. And *that* is the cornerstone of successful interviewing—self-confidence.

If you have done your homework, you are now ready to learn how to make "the big pitch." In sales, it's called a sales presentation. In a job search, it's called an *interview.* The result of a successful sales presentation is a sale. The result of a successful interview is also a sale, spelled *j-o-b.* When you have completed this chapter you should look forward to the challenge of clinching the sale. You have carefully and systematically prepared for this moment of triumph. It's time to get ready to savor the sweet taste of job search success.

Philosophy

What is an interview . . . an interrogation? No. Although some interviewers may try to grill you—don't let them. Grilling is for raw meat, not people. Neither should an interview be a monologue, by you or by the interviewer. Nor should it be two monologues, one following another.

An ideal interview takes the form of a dialogue or conversation. It involves a business-like exchange of necessary information between two parties (and oftentimes more). It is a conversation with both parties asking and answering questions that are pertinent to the successful performance of the job at stake. And, of no less importance, it should be a mutual attempt to determine how happily you, your boss, and your employer might coexist in a prolonged relationship.

As experienced and as qualified as a candidate might be, in too many instances it is the candidate who *gets along best* with the interviewer that wins the job. This assumes, of course, that this candidate possesses enough qualifications to suggest he or she can handle the position.

Sometimes, all it takes is to uncover one item of common interest and the chances for success increase considerably. Many resume experts will tell you that hobbies or personal interests have no place on a resume. Not always true. Many times, a mutual or unusual hobby or interest can promote a dialogue between you and the interviewer. Consider how many people play golf, love sports, or travel. Discovering an item of mutual interest oftentimes helps to dissolve the invisible wall separating the two parties.

Interview Preparation

A successful interview begins with researching the company and the position you seek. If possible, talk to people who work at, or know about, the company.

We're going to be talking about interview questions later in this chapter. The pre-interview research you have conducted should prompt some intelligent questions you should be ready to ask the interviewer. Now, before you're under the gun, is the time to work on both the questions to be ready to answer and those to be ready to ask. Good questions go a long way toward promoting a dialogue.

Once you have the information you need and are ready to interview, be certain you know how to get to the interview location and how long it will take to get there. Be sure to allow for unexpected delays such as a traffic jam, a flat tire, or an unexpected detour. Look the location up on a map. Call the company and ask for specific directions. If it's not too far away, make a practice run just to be safe. Make sure you have the interviewer's telephone number when you leave the house that day. If something goes awry, be sure to call and explain your predicament.

Dress

Blue suits, gray suits, pant suits, "power" ties, vests, no vests. There are entire books written on this subject. If you are really that uncertain how to dress for an interview you might like to read one of them. But there's a quicker way to determine what dress would be appropriate for a particular interview.

If in doubt, call the company. Tell the receptionist you have an interview in the such-and-such department and ask how the people in that department dress. Still not sure? Follow this axiom: except in rare situations, it's safer to be conservatively rather than flamboyantly attired.

Appearance

Good personal hygiene and appearance is important, but if you don't know this by now you probably don't care. Hair and clothing must be clean, neat, and professional. When in doubt, go for a classic, conservative look.

A word of caution about perfumes, colognes, or after-shave lotions. Go easy. Don't load up and overpower your interviewer. Some people are actually allergic to certain scents. There's no way you will have a successful interview if all the interviewer wants to do is to get you and your perfume out of his or her office as quickly as possible.

Don't overload on jewelry. Shine your shoes, if they need it. Try to be honest with yourself when you look in the mirror. Would *you* like to work closely, every day, with the person you see there? Would *you* hire the person looking back at you?

Interview Folio

Bring along a folio when you interview. Include in it:

- A note pad, two or three erasable pens, and a pocket dictionary.
- Several extra resumes and reference sheets.

- The originals, and copies, of letters of recommendation.
- Recent educational transcripts and course catalogs, if you are a recent college graduate
- Portfolio ("Show and Tell" for big kids).

References

This is a very important topic; one to which too many job seekers pay too little attention. References can make or break your candidacy.

The Reference Process

1. Who to Select
   - People who know you and can speak convincingly about your experiences, attributes, and accomplishments.
   - Your most recent and former employers, supervisors, and management personnel.
   - Your peers and subordinates.
2. How to Ask Permission
   - In person or by phone.
   - Hold a general discussion on appropriate reference answers.
   - Discuss the approach you will take with dispensing references: that you will give out the reference's contact information upon request only.
   - Assure your references that you will contact them regarding forthcoming reference checks.
3. Develop a Termination Statement
   - If you were terminated from your last position, try to reach an agreement with your former supervisor on what he or she will tell prospective future employers about your employment and termination.
   - Draft the statement and forward a copy to your former supervisor for his or her signature, if possible.
   - Provide any other references at the company with copies of this statement so that they too will be prepared to respond to inquiries.

4. Ask Your References to Critique Your Resume
   - Discuss and critique your resume with appropriate references.
   - Provide all references with a finished copy.
5. Contact and Update Your References Periodically
   - Let them know how your search is progressing.
   - Discuss improvements you have made to your resume.
   - Ask for new leads.
   - Tell them what person and/or employer might contact them.
   - Describe the position under consideration.
   - Elaborate on the job requirements.
   - Remind them how your experiences and background fit the position. Ask them to call back with their feedback after being contacted.
6. Contact Yet Again at the Conclusion of Your Job Search
   - Describe the position you have accepted.
   - Thank them for their support.

If you intend to have a list of references to hand out upon request, it should be listed on a separate matching sheet of stationery. Type your name, address, and telephone number at the top of the paper. Then type in caps, centered at the top of the page, "REFERENCES." Skip down a few lines and type the contact information for each reference. List four or five references. Include, if given permission, the telephone numbers where they may be reached during normal working hours. *Never list a reference without first seeking permission.* As your search progresses, be certain your contact information is kept up-to-date and your references advised of your progress.

Remember the Rule of Seven? (See Chapter 4, "How to Develop, Contact, and Pursue Job Leads.") Now's the time to use it. Although you will never use them all, you can ask anyone you know if they would be kind enough to act as a reference. Asking people if they would be willing to serve as a reference is yet another way of building and maintaining your network.

One final warning about selecting your references. Be as certain as you possibly can that they will have good things to say about you . . . something more substantial than, "She's a wonderful person."

Letters of Recommendation

Letters of recommendation can be an even better way of backing up your candidacy. Instead of relying on what someone *might say,* they show both you and an interviewer what the person *has already said.* Obtain at least two or three letters. When asked at the interview if you have any references, show the letters instead. It's a lot quicker, impressive, and sometimes safer. Take along copies of each letter in case you are asked to leave the letters with the interviewer. Recognize that some employers may still prefer to telephone your references and talk to them directly.

Portfolio Materials: "Show and Tell" for Big Kids

A Picture's Worth a Thousand Words

A typical interview consists of words, words, and more words. That's fine for your competition, but certainly not for you. You don't want to have a "typical" interview. You want to SOAR above the competition. Here's a way for you to have technicolor interviews while your competition's still appearing in black and white—use visuals.

Gather together as many of the following materials as you can:

- Samples of outstanding, nonproprietary, work you have done.
- Superior performance appraisal ratings.
- Sales literature from your last employer, the employer doing the interviewing, and this employer's competitors, if applicable.
- Annual reports.
- Directory information about the employer: size, sales, products/services, locations, etc.
- Newspaper/magazine articles about the employer, the industry, the interviewer, and the competition, if applicable.
- Statistics about the community and its makeup (if considering relocation).

Now, make several copies of the materials you have gathered together. Highlight those sections of this information you would like to discuss or ask questions about. Place all of these materials in a file folder with the employer's name on it. Place a copy of your resume on the top of this pile.

At the interview, immediately following introductions, reach into your briefcase and withdraw this file. Remove your resume and offer it to the employer . . . even if he or she has already received one. Why? You want to be interviewed off of your resume. It can act as a road map for the journey ahead—and you drew the map.

Withdrawing the file folder, and then your resume from it, gives you a chance to surreptitiously place the folder on your lap—please, *not* on the employer's desk! Here are a few reasons for playing "Show and Tell" for big kids:

- When the interviewer sees the file, he or she will become curious as to what else you might have tucked away in your "goody grab bag."
- It indicates that you have done your homework and want to avoid wasting the interviewer's valuable time and yours.
- It indicates the type of due diligence the interviewer might expect you to bring to the position for which you are interviewing.

"Show and Tell" for big kids is a wonderful way to add color to the interview process. Not only this, but you will feel more prepared and comfortable for whatever may lie ahead. Using "Show and Tell" can influence the direction the interview will take. When you can do this, you are well on your way to interviewing success.

If you want to win the job of your dreams you absolutely cannot afford to be just another face in the crowd. "Show and Tell" and rise above the masses.

Get Ready to SOAR

You have used your SOAR statements of accomplishments (see Chapter 1, "How to Leave the Competition in the Dust") in your cover letters, resumes, and telephone conversations. They should be second nature to you by now, but don't take anything for granted. Continue to rehearse and perfect them. There is no other pre-interview activity as important as building and rehearsing powerful SOAR statements.

The Answer and Ask Technique

The answer and ask technique is used to promote a dialogue by attempting to avert your becoming a victim of the traditional interrogation-style interview. You know, the one where you sit under the naked light bulb, have smoke blown in your face, and attempt to answer a barrage of questions. Suddenly, the barrage lifts unexpectedly. You are asked if you have any questions you'd like to ask. Completely rattled and emotionally drained, you reply: "Yes. How much does this position pay?," "What are the benefits?," or "How much vacation time do I get?"

These are all very legitimate, need-to-know questions. But they are certainly not the most appropriate ones to begin with because you project a "What's in it for me?" attitude, rather than a "What can I do *for you?*" attitude.

Here's how the answer and ask strategy works: The interviewer asks you a question. You answer it, in no more than one minute, using a SOAR statement. Let's suppose you have been asked that old interview favorite:

"Tell me about yourself."

You answer:

"One of my most recent accomplishments that pertains to this position is <u>*(whatever)*</u> *."*

This accomplishment becomes the subject of the SOAR statement that follows.

Then, at the conclusion of your SOAR statement (your answer), you ask . . . "Is that the type of information you are looking for?" A question as innocuous as this will certainly elicit a response such as:

"That's fine, but I would really like to learn a little more about your <u>*(whatever)*</u> *."*

By asking questions, you begin to break down the wall some interviewers place between you and themselves. By following many of your answers with questions, you take the first step toward creating a mutually productive dialogue. Both the interviewer and you must have the opportunity to discover whether or not this "marriage" you are considering is in the best interest of the both of you.

Too many job seekers are delighted to land a job, only to discover the job they've landed, or the boss that hired them, is not compatible. Now, they have a painful decision to make—either stay on and grin and bear it or leave and begin another job search. Answer and ask. Find out as much as you can about the employer and the working conditions before you're offered, and blindly accept, the position.

In practicing your SOAR statements, be sure to conclude each with a question for the interviewer. Naturally, the question must have some connection with the topic you have just talked about. At the interview, don't attempt to conclude *every* answer with a question. Just remain alert and prepared for opportunities to answer and ask.

Role-Playing

Do some interview role-playing. Get together with a friend or loved one and have her fire questions at you. The two of you should try to be as objective and constructively critical of your answers as possible. Were they positive? Were they believable? Were they to the point? Did they portray you as someone who could contribute to the company? Someone whom others would enjoy working with or for? Did you back up and validate your claims with specific, results oriented, SOAR statements? No? Then go back to the drawing board.

Such things as good eye contact, positive attitude, and using SOAR statements can be practiced with another person through interview role playing. You can also practice these techniques and skills in your daily contact with people. They'll never know you're doing it. After you get one technique or skill "down pat" start working on perfecting a new one.

The Pre-Interview

Arrive at the interview location early, but don't walk into the office until just a few minutes before the scheduled time. If it looks like you're going to be late, get to a phone and let the employer know.

Once you arrive on company grounds, greet everyone you meet with a friendly smile and a "hello." That person who almost ran you down as you got out of your car in the parking lot might be your interviewer hurrying to your interview.

You arrive at the interviewer's office just a few minutes before your appointment time. Why? Because, if asked to do so, you don't want to fill out an application until after your interview. Being just a trifle early, perhaps won't give you the time required to fill one out before the interview begins.

Be certain you know how to pronounce and spell your interviewer's name. If you don't know how he or she prefers to be addressed, ask the secretary. Also be certain you know the interviewer's title. Once you have verified this information ask if there is a rest room nearby where you can freshen up. Use the rest room mirror to give yourself a once-over. Check your appearance carefully—no dandruff on the collar, mussed-up hair, makeup askew, or crooked tie.

Application Guidelines

When you are interviewed off of your resume, rather than an application, you have a better idea of, and are more likely to play a part in, the direction the interview might take. Therefore, you'd rather *not* fill out an application before the interview. However, if you do have to complete an application, read it over before putting erasable pen to paper.

Yes, erasable pen. How many times have you completed any form without making some sort of mistake? It says to print, you start in writing. It asks for last name first, you write in your first name first. Become the world's first job search candidate to complete an application without visibly goofing up. Use an erasable pen. Here are some more guidelines to follow:

1. Read the directions carefully before printing your answers.
2. Complete the form exactly as instructed. *Example:* Please Print: Last Name, First Name, Middle Initial.
3. Never falsify an answer or response. Never leave a blank space if a response is called for. If there is a question you feel will jeopardize your chances for the position, you have three choices:
   - Fill it in truthfully and pray.
   - Draw a line (———) in the space. Be prepared to address this question later, if given the chance.

- Write in "NA" (not applicable) if you feel the question is really out of bounds. Once again, be prepared to answer for your response or to be rejected without comment.

Interview Checklist

The items included on this list are self-explanatory. Before an interview, spend a few minutes reviewing each one so you can incorporate as many as possible, logically, into the interview process. A weakness in any one of these areas could be enough to ruin your chances. If, for example, you do not know very much about the company you are interviewing with, you are definitely not ready for the interview. Your chances for success will be minimal.

Constructive self-criticism is the key to improved interviews. Be prepared. Review the following checklist before each and every interview. Immediately following each interview, as soon as you can, review it again.

If you own a small cassette recorder, now, when you get back to your car, is the time to use it. Review the interview in your mind. Did you meet the criteria? Could you have done better? How? During the ride back home, keep mulling the interview over in your mind looking for places where you could have been stronger, or where you think you really scored points. Think about the thank-you note you will send and what you can say in it to further advance your cause.

Vow right now that you will mail a thank-you note immediately after every interview.

The Checklist

1. Be on time.
2. Dress appropriately.
3. Bring a folio.
4. Know the interviewer's name, pronunciation, spelling—know the interviewer's title—Dr., Mr., Miss, Mrs., or Ms.
5. Extend a warm greeting and handshake—smile!
6. Wait to be asked to be seated.
7. Maintain good eye contact.
8. Be enthusiastic.
9. Have a good knowledge of the company, industry, position, interviewer, and job location.
10. Be ready to answer questions.
11. Be ready to ask questions.

If you're prepared on all of the above points, you're ready to have a good interview. You'll also find it's a lot easier to get a good night's sleep the night before an interview when you've done your homework.

The Interview

You're called into the interviewer's office. You greet him or her with a smile and a warm, firm, handshake. You wait to be asked to be seated. If you have a choice between a seat directly opposite the interviewer and one diagonal to him, choose the latter. It helps physically and psychologically to reduce the "space" between the two of you. Offer him a resume, even if he already received one. You want to be interviewed off of the document you created and not off of the application, if possible. Look him squarely in the eye. Act enthusiastic, motivated, and intense.

Your responses to questions are positive, considered, and concise. When you don't understand the question, you ask to have it rephrased. Sometimes, when you *do* know what the question means, you still ask to have it rephrased. This gives you time to come up with a good answer. You ask insightful, pertinent questions about the job, the employer, and your prospective boss. You judiciously dispense knowledge obtained through research conducted prior to the interview.

Whenever possible and relevant, you back up your answers with brief, specific examples. After answering a question, you might ask: "Is that the type of information you are looking for?" You're not afraid to pause to take the time to think before answering tough questions. If you don't know the answer to a question, just admit it.

Through it all, no matter how well you and the interviewer are getting along, one thought remains foremost in your thoughts and directs your answers, "Sell. Sell. Sell. Show why I should be hired." In fact, the better you and the interviewer hit it off, the more likely you may be to start to confess and complain. If an interviewer asks you to sit around a coffee table, "because it's more comfortable," you'll know that you're about to interact with a skilled interviewer.

Finally, be aware of your body language and eye contact. Do not slouch back in the chair. Instead, sit comfortably upright, slightly on the edge of the seat. Lean forward slightly when receiving or imparting particularly important or interesting information. *Do not gesticulate wildly with your hands. Do* use them to punctuate points you wish to make. Finally, look the interviewer in the eye without attempting to hypnotize him.

Face-to-Face

It is impossible to list all of the things that could transpire sitting opposite an interviewer. Fortunately, there are a few situations that do occur repeatedly. Expect to find variations on the following themes:

- You and the interviewer do not "hit it off." For whatever reason, you cannot stand one another. Or, maybe the company, in your estimation, has turned out to be a real loser. Don't rush for the door. Bite your tongue. Ask politely if he might be kind enough to suggest another possible lead.
- You and the interviewer "hit it off" but . . . she really cannot hire you. Thank her for her time. Make sure she has your resume. Ask if she could suggest another lead. Tell her if you're still on the market a few weeks from now you intend to call her to see if anything might have opened up since you last talked. After all, her company is the company that you have your heart set on joining . . . isn't it?
- You and the interviewer "hit it off." He likes you enough to search for ways to justify adding you to his team. Now several exciting possibilities open up. If he doesn't bring them up you might suggest them tactfully.

He could try to hire you by:

- Placing you in an existing but unadvertised opening.
- Slotting you to fill an upcoming opening.
- Finding a temporary opening for you to fill until the job you want opens up.
- Creating an opening for you by releasing an unproductive or problem employee currently holding the position you're seeking.
- Offering you a consulting assignment.
- Or, he might recommend you to another employer or business acquaintance.

Questions, Questions

A good interview involves give-and-take. You're shopping the company and the company is shopping you. It is possible the questions you've been asked during an interview will help you to decide you really don't want the job after all—*better to find out now than after you start working.*

Conversely, your replies to an interviewer's questions may lead him to decide you're not right for the position, the company, or his team. Whether you might like to admit it or not, he's probably correct in his assessment. After all, he knows the company and the position much better than you do. Consider this: *in rejecting you, he could very well be doing you a favor.*

Never Confess, Never Complain

No one will ever hire a complainer. Companies already have enough moaners and groaners. Be positive. If you can't say something good about a person, an institution, or an employer, don't say anything!

Above all, you should know by now that the key word is *profit* and the key question is, *"Why should I hire you?"* Study the following questions. You will undoubtedly be asked, or will ask, all of them sooner or later in your interviews. Be positive in your answers. Use SOAR statements. Practice following each answer with a question. Answer and ask.

Four Approaches to Answering Questions

Before looking at the types of questions you will likely be asked, let's examine the four approaches you can use in answering them. I'm not talking about the content of your answers, but rather the mode you adopt to answer them.

Direct Response. This is the most common approach. We use it automatically. You are asked the question and you answer it, in a straightforward manner.

With a Question. If you don't understand the question asked, you ask if the interviewer would be kind enough to restate it. That's one reason you use a question approach. Another reason is to lead the interviewer away from the question he or she is expecting an answer to and onto a different but related topic for which you have a stronger response. Example:

Interviewer:	*What kind of money are you looking for?*
You:	*That's a good question but I really don't know enough about the position to give you an intelligent answer. What are the possibilities for advancement with this position?*

Non-Response. This could just as easily be called the "political response." See if you recognize this approach. Rather than answer the question asked in a weak or negative fashion, you try to tactfully avoid it by continuing on with the dialogue. For example, let's suppose you were fired from your last position:

Interviewer:	*Why did you leave the company you were with?*
You:	*As you probably know, the company has been undergoing a lot of changes. The whole industry, like so many others today, has adopted this same mode. I've been doing some reading about your company and wonder why you haven't been as hard hit as your competitors . . . (Now, ask.) . . . to what do you attribute your success?*

Humorous. This is a great way to break the ice, but it can also prove to be treacherous—especially if your interviewer has no sense of humor or doesn't appreciate your trying to be humorous. Here's how one candidate responded to a question and received a laugh:

Interviewer:	*What would you say your greatest weakness is?*
Interviewee:	*Impatience. Next question?*

Or, consider how my wife used humor to her advantage when being interviewed about a possible promotion:

Interviewer:	*I see that you have three young children. The position we are talking about calls for you to be on the road two or three nights a week. What would you do with your children?*

This was definitely an illegal question, and she knew it. But instead of reacting negatively, she hesitated, smiled, and replied: "I'm sure I could sell two of them, but the third one we might have to give away . . . But seriously, yes, I am available for overnight travel two or three nights a week."

If you discover your interviewer has a sense of humor, cautiously join in the fun, but don't go overboard and don't lower your guard.

Humor is also a great tool for getting you to confess and complain without your realizing it. If you enjoy humor, but are reluctant to try it, you're probably better off to smile as much as you can and dispense with witticisms.

Questions to Answer

Here are few of the more commonly asked interview questions. I've included sample responses for those questions job seekers sometimes need help in answering.

1. Tell me all about yourself.

   This is probably the most commonly asked opening interview question. Most job seekers reply in the following manner:

   "Well, I graduated in 1972 from Clifton University with a degree in Mechanical Engineering. My first position was with Samson Steel. While at Samson I was ... "

   There is nothing wrong with this conventional response except that it is a *conventional, run-of-the-mill response.* You have worked long and hard on your SOAR statements. Now's the time to SOAR, to begin taxiing down the runway:

   "I have several strong points I am proud of. Perhaps my greatest strength is my problem solving ability."

   You have just begun a SOAR statement with "problem solving ability" being the subject of this statement. You continue on:

   "We had a situation not too long ago ..."

   Now you have begun the overview section of the SOAR statement. Next, you relate the action you took followed by the results of this action. You conclude your response with a question, such as:

   "Is this the type of information you are looking for?"

   By asking such an innocuous question at the top of the interview, you attempt to set the pattern for the interview.

Bear in mind, the most productive interviews are dialogues, not interrogations.

_____

_____

_____

2. Why should we hire you?

   Here is another perfect opportunity to present a SOAR statement.

_____

_____

_____

3. What are your career goals? Five years from now? Ten years? Ultimately?

_____

_____

_____

4. What is your definition of success?

_____

_____

_____

5. Tell me about yourself. What are your strong points?

   Here is a perfect opportunity for yet another SOAR statement. Just be aware that this is almost always part one of a two-part question; the other part being question #6.

_____

_____

_____

6. What are your weak points?

   Never confess. Never complain. Saying you have no weak points is ludicrous. But saying what they are can sometimes be almost as bad. Try to make a statement that sounds like a weak point but is, in fact, a strong point.

"I am a perfectionist. It often drives me and everybody around me crazy at times. I just can't be satisfied until the job is done properly in every way."

_____

_____

_____

7. Why did you go into _____(your career choice)_____?

_____

_____

_____

8. If I called your last boss, what might he or she have to tell me about you?

What happens if you, like some of us, didn't get along particularly well with your most recent boss (or any boss)? You already know that you are never to confess nor complain. You have to answer the question at hand in as positive a manner as possible. What about something like this:

"I can't speak for my past boss or any other person, but I hope he would tell you that . . ."

And now you launch into a SOAR statement, such as:

"I have an excellent ability to analyze situations."

That was the opening subject part of the SOAR statement that you will then proceed to relate. Now you embark upon the overview portion of the SOAR statement.

"Not too long ago the _____ department was faced with a dilemma. It seems that . . ." (etc.)

_____

_____

_____

9. What do you look for when hiring subordinates?

_____

_____

_____

10. Why are you interested in working for our company?

Unless you're responding to an ad or have been referred by a headhunter, you can't possibly answer this question effectively if you haven't done any homework about the employer and its products or services. And, if you have done your homework, now is the time to shine.

_"I've been studying your most recent annual report. I was most impressed by your development of the CYX Automaton. I've been working in robotics research and implementation for the past five years. One of the things that should interest you, is my experience with the _____."_

_____

_____

_____

11. What were your most rewarding and disappointing educational or work experiences?

Telling the most rewarding experience should be easy enough to do, especially if you have a SOAR statement or two to go along with it. However, telling the most disappointing experience could open up a Pandora's box you might not be able to close.

_____

_____

_____

12. What have you learned from your work experiences?

_____

_____

_____

13. What is your greatest accomplishment?

_____

_____

_____

14. Why do you want to work for us?

Unless you know a good deal about the employer, you probably won't know why, or even if, you want to work for him. Rather than to try to come up with some petty answer, why not reply:

"Quite frankly, I don't know enough about the company to answer that question intelligently. (Pulling out the annual report, if applicable) I've been doing some homework. Would you mind answering a few questions I have ... ?"

_____

_____

_____

15. What do you expect from an employer?

Be careful. It's better to show and ask the employer what *you* can do for him or her. Employers don't offer handouts just to keep employees happy—especially ones yet to be hired.

_____

_____

_____

16. What have you done to advance in your field?

What if your answer is "nothing"? How do you think that will make you look? But you have to answer the question, even if you really haven't been doing anything to better yourself. You might try to respond in this way:

"Well," you reply, "I haven't really had the time to do all of the things I would like to do. I look upon this job change as an opportunity to really advance my career."

It may be appropriate to reach into your briefcase and withdraw a college or seminar catalog. As you do so you say:

"I've been doing a little research and have narrowed my choices for possible courses (or seminars) down to three or four." (Which you have highlighted in yellow magic marker in the catalog.)

"I would really appreciate your input as to the ones most pertinent to the position we are discussing. Would you mind taking a quick glance at them? I have them highlighted."

You won't find very many interviewers who can resist the opportunity to show you what they know.

_____

_____

_____

17. Why did you choose the major you did?

_____

_____

_____

18. What was your class rank in college?

_____

_____

_____

19. What types of activities are you involved in?

_____

_____

_____

20. What do you do in your spare time?

_____

_____

_____

21. What makes you think you are qualified for this position?

"As I understand it, you're looking for someone who can _____. I have that experience. I mentioned I _____ (repeating a SOAR statement you made earlier) _____."

And then you ask:

"Am I accurate in describing the position? Did I miss something or leave something out?"

_____

_____

_____

22. Is there anything else I should know about you?

_____

_____

_____

23. How much money are you looking for?
    If you can possibly avoid it, never discuss money or benefits until the end of an interview, or even better yet at a future interview. You will soon see why and how to try to avoid answering this question prematurely.

_____

_____

_____

24. Who do you admire the most? Why?

_____

_____

_____

25. What do you look for in a subordinate?

_____

_____

_____

26. What is your operating style?

_____

_____

_____

27. How do you handle problem employees or problem situations?

_____

_____

_____

28. What do you do if you can't find the answer to a problem?

_____

_____

_____

29. How soon can you start?

_____

_____

_____

30. What is your definition of job satisfaction?

"Looking forward to going to work each day. Knowing that my associates look forward to working with me each day. Getting along with everyone but especially with my immediate supervisor."

Answer, then ask:

"Which leads me to ask, would you be my immediate supervisor?"

_____

_____

_____

Pause to consider your answers. Keep your answers brief and to the point. Don't talk indiscriminately! *Listen to what the interviewer is saying.* Don't interrupt. Be careful when you are trying to change the subject. However, if the interviewer is hitting upon a weak area, you must try to lead him or her into greener pastures. This is another reason why asking questions is so important. If you have been asking them all along, it won't seem too obvious if you ask one or two more to try to subtly change the subject under discussion.

Questions to Ask

Following are some questions you should consider asking to make each interview a true give-and-take situation. And then, upon receiving an offer, you will have solicited the information needed to make a sensible, reasoned, and informed decision. Again, look for statements or questions on which you might "piggyback" your questions.

1. Why is the position open? How long has it been open? (Is there something wrong with the position? Now is the time to find out. If you aren't satisfied with the response don't hesitate, dig a little deeper.)
2. What happened to the previous job holder? Has he been promoted? (Does this mean it can happen to you? How? How soon?)
3. What is the career path associated with this position?

4. Who would be my boss? Can I meet her? What is her background?
5. What is your management philosophy?
6. How, by whom, and how often, would my performance be evaluated?
7. Where would my work area or office be? Can I see it?
8. Something in my resume must have captured your interest. Would you mind sharing that with me? (The answer can reveal what it is they are really interested in.)
9. What is the company's posture in the marketplace?
10. What are some problems in my area of interest?
11. What is the company's practice regarding salary increases? Promotions?
12. Who would I be working with? Who would be working for me?
13. What is the chain of command?
14. How often do you have staff meetings? Is there an agenda?
15. Would you mind sharing a little of your background with me?
16. What are the benefits? Are there any waiting periods? (These two final questions should be held in abeyance until the end of the interview or better yet until a follow-up interview.)
17. What is the salary range or salary? Is the salary negotiable?

Illegal Interview Questions

You should not be asked the following questions. *They're illegal.* However, interviewers who lack knowledge or training may ask them anyway, so be prepared.

- How old are you? (Can be answered after you are hired.)
- What is your year of birth? (Can be answered after you are hired.)
- Do you attend church? Which one?
- Do you have an arrest record? (Security clearance can be conducted prior to hiring.)
- What type of military discharge did you get?
- What clubs and organizations are you a member of?

- What is your marital status? Are you divorced? Separated? (Can be answered after hiring, for insurance purposes.)
- Do you have any children? What are their ages?
- Do you own a car? (Can be asked regarding transportation to a job.)
- Do you own or rent a home?
- What does your spouse do for a living?
- What was your maiden name?
- What is your race?

How to Handle Illegal Questions

You don't *have* to answer these questions, but you may volunteer an answer or two if you feel that doing so won't violate your integrity and might bolster your candidacy. For example, suppose the position involves travel and overnight stays away from home. Obviously an employer would never hire a person for such a position if it might cause problems at home. In this instance, you might volunteer that you ". . . do own a car, enjoy traveling, and, being single, don't need to be concerned with problems or ties back home."

When an employer asks you an illegal question, it can present you with a definite predicament. Perhaps you don't mind answering the question, but you may resent the fact that the interviewer asked. You might feel if you avoid answering the question your chances of getting the job will be greatly reduced.

What can you do? While there is no guaranteed strategy, here are several options:

- You can walk out and forget about the job.
- You can walk out, forget about the job, and file a complaint with the appropriate federal or state agency.
- You can inform the interviewer that he has no right to ask such a question.
- You can answer it.
- You can smile and place the ball back in his court (just as my wife did).

The Money Question

Try to put off answering the money question until late in the interview, or even until a second interview. The question of money is often used as a screening device. If you are asked early on, "What do you expect to make in this position?" the answer you give may decide the length of the ensuing interview. If you want too much or not enough, the interview is apt to be very brief. Also remember, if you do a good job of selling yourself you should always be worth more in the employer's eyes at the end of the interview than at the beginning.

Avoid Stating a Salary Figure

Here are a few ways you can attempt to avoid the money question, should it arise prematurely during interviews. Here is the avoidance tactic I like the best:

> "Don't misunderstand me, money's very important; but it's not my number one priority. I want a job that fits my skills and abilities. Can you tell me a little more about the managerial responsibilities?"

Another avoidance tactic, and this also concludes with an essential question, is to reply:

> "That's a good question, but I really can't answer it at this juncture. I don't have enough information about this particular position. Can you tell me a little more about the managerial responsibilities?"

Always conclude your answer with a question as closely related to the money question as possible, but one that can still make the interviewer forget the exact question he or she has asked. Later, after you've sold yourself, maybe not until a second interview, you turn to him or her and ask:

> "I know I can do a great job for you in this position. What kind of money are we talking about?"

Don't think for one minute that an experienced interviewer will let you get away with these avoidance tactics. If you are forced to state a figure, do so, but be certain it is realistic. Do some research to find out the going rate for your position. If you're in doubt, don't underprice yourself. You can always come down in price, but it's almost impossible to go up.

When pressed for a figure, some candidates respond: "Fifty to fifty-five."

You can bet, unless he has to, the interviewer will never offer this person fifty-five immediately. Why not? Because the candidate wasn't making fifty-five; that's what he is *hoping* to make. Would he ever have given fifty as one of the two figures if he was making fifty-five? Nobody looks for less than they were making in their last position! A better idea is to state an approximate figure such as "the mid sixties," or, "right around fifty."

In a successful interview, you will want to make yourself look more valuable to the interviewer as the interview progresses. As you heighten his interest, you simultaneously heighten the price tag he will expect to have to pay to get you. A successful candidate is always worth more at the conclusion of an interview than at the beginning. If possible, put off talking about money until the moment appears to be right.

Negotiating Additional Income

Once again, the best time to talk money is *after* you've sold yourself. When the employer is convinced you can help him or her make more money or solve a particular problem, he or she will be more willing to negotiate with you.

Another thing to consider, if you can, is whether or not the figure you're seeking is going to be too much or too little. If it's likely to be too much, you can omit mentioning any bonuses or commissions you received beyond and above your base salary. If it looks like this figure is not enough, you can add bonuses, commissions, and perks to it to build it up.

Some positions have a set salary. It cannot be negotiated. If you encounter a situation such as this you should attempt to negotiate some additional perks or benefits; items such as: a company car, a car allowance, a travel allowance, stock options, professional memberships, a bonus plan, and so on.

When trying to decide whether or not you can afford to take a position offered you, don't forget to keep in mind some other considerations: state and local taxes, educational expenses, living expenses, housing expenses, etc. Also keep in mind the opportunity for advancement. Accepting less than you would like to now, could actually lead to earning more in the future.

OFFER EVALUATION CHECKLIST

Job Considerations	Yes	No	NA
Know company history	❏	❏	❏
Know company objectives/plans	❏	❏	❏
Have seen annual report/10-K/news articles	❏	❏	❏
Interviewed prospective boss	❏	❏	❏
Know management philosophy/style	❏	❏	❏
Know frequency of staff meetings	❏	❏	❏
Know meeting format	❏	❏	❏
Have seen written job description	❏	❏	❏
Know when it was written	❏	❏	❏
Met fellow employees/subordinates	❏	❏	❏
Have seen work area	❏	❏	❏
Know company tree	❏	❏	❏
Know where position can lead to	❏	❏	❏
Know how soon	❏	❏	❏
Know performance appraisal criteria	❏	❏	❏
Know frequency of performance appraisal	❏	❏	❏
Know if results can be appealed/contested	❏	❏	❏
Know how such action is handled	❏	❏	❏
Know extent of travel	❏	❏	❏
Know starting date	❏	❏	❏

Living Considerations—Are you familiar with:	Yes	No	NA
Cost of living	❑	❑	❑
Local/state taxes	❑	❑	❑
Commuting time	❑	❑	❑
Educational opportunities	❑	❑	❑
Health care facilities	❑	❑	❑
Recreational facilities/activities	❑	❑	❑
Security conditions	❑	❑	❑
Income Considerations—Have you discussed/negotiated:			
Bonus	❑	❑	❑
Car allowance	❑	❑	❑
Educational allowance	❑	❑	❑
Relocation allowance	❑	❑	❑
Health insurance	❑	❑	❑
Dental/optical insurance	❑	❑	❑
Disability insurance	❑	❑	❑
Salary review	❑	❑	❑
Pension plan	❑	❑	❑
Deferred income	❑	❑	❑
Profit sharing	❑	❑	❑
Stock options	❑	❑	❑
Cost-of-living adjustment	❑	❑	❑
Paid vacation	❑	❑	❑
Expense account	❑	❑	❑
Employment contract	❑	❑	❑
Severance benefits	❑	❑	❑

	Yes	No	NA
Professional/Club memberships	❏	❏	❏
Salary continuation	❏	❏	❏
Benefits continuation	❏	❏	❏
Perks continuation	❏	❏	❏
Outplacement	❏	❏	❏
Immediate vesting	❏	❏	❏
Relocation Considerations—Have you included:			
Cost of temporary living	❏	❏	❏
Trips back home	❏	❏	❏
House hunting trips	❏	❏	❏
House options	❏	❏	❏
Bridge loan for new house	❏	❏	❏
Broker's fees for sale	❏	❏	❏
Packing/loading/transport	❏	❏	❏
Special items (boat/car)	❏	❏	❏
Unhook/hookups	❏	❏	❏
Expenses en route	❏	❏	❏
Gross up for taxes	❏	❏	❏
Spouse placement	❏	❏	❏

Stalling for Time

You may receive an offer and not be quite certain whether to accept it or not. Perhaps you have a more promising one "in the wings." Perhaps it involves relocating and you would prefer to find something locally. (Incidentally, never turn down an interview because you don't want to relocate. Every once in awhile, an employer that is interviewing out of your area will have a facility, or will need a representative, right in your own backyard. If the employer likes you, he or she won't want to lose you.)

Here are a few stalling tactics for your consideration:

- Ask how soon an answer is needed.
- Ask how soon you can expect "to see something in writing."
- Bargain with the employer over the terms of the contract.
- Say you appreciate the offer and need to talk it over with the family.

I once heard an employer say he would never hire a person who had to get his spouse's approval before accepting the job. My own feeling is quite contrary. I believe it is a considerate and thoughtful job hunter who involves family in a decision that will likely have a dramatic impact upon their lifestyle.

Occasionally, an employer will insist on an immediate answer. This presents a most difficult situation. Even if you have no other promising leads, you should be very careful before accepting an offer under these terms.

The question you must ask yourself is, "Why?" Why do they want an immediate commitment? Is it a "no-win" position? Are they in financial or technical trouble? Is the boss a tough person to work for?

There is absolutely nothing wrong with asking an employer why he is insistent on receiving an immediate decision. If he hesitates in responding, or if his response raises more questions than it answers, you would be well advised to turn the offer down, if you can afford to.

If you really need a job and the employer demands an immediate answer, say yes. Then, should something better come along, change your mind or give your notice. I know it's not a very nice thing to do. However, I don't know about you, but I have little sympathy for someone who tries to take advantage of another person's dilemma.

You can sense the interview drawing to a close. You may be relieved, but this is no time to drop your guard. There is one more definite action you must take.

The Last Question

As you prepare to exit the interview, you should always say and ask the following:

"I really enjoyed meeting you and finding out more about how I could con-tribute to your bottom line. Where do we go from here?"

Never walk away from an interview without a commitment or a new lead. The basic rule of prospecting is to *always use one lead to develop another*. If you don't, you'll wake up one morning out of leads and down in the dumps. Without generating new leads each and every day your campaign will end up bankrupt. That's a situation to be avoided at all costs.

If things didn't go as well as you might have liked during the interview, be certain to ask:

"I'm sorry things didn't work out. Maybe you would be kind enough to sug-gest someone else I should talk to? Might I use your name when I call?"

You must come away from every contact you make, by phone or in person, with a new name, address, or telephone number. Or, at the very least, the name of an employer your original contact might be able to provide. *Always use one lead to develop another.* (See Chapter 4, "How to Develop, Contact, and Pursue Job Leads.") Also, be certain to ask if you might use the interviewer's name when contacting the reference given you.

When You Are Turned Down

If you really felt you had the inside track on a position you didn't get, don't just roll over and play dead. Pick up the phone and call the interviewer. Politely ask if he might be kind enough to tell you why you were rejected. Tell him you're not calling to try to get him to change his mind or to argue with him. You would really appre-ciate any constructive criticism he might be willing to share with you. It will help you to better prepare for future interviews. Sometimes this is all it takes to renew interest in your candidacy—especially if you were the runner-up and the person they selected didn't work out.

Interview Assessment Record

There are some definite things to keep in mind so that you will con-stantly improve at the interview game. You don't have to be a pro-fessional job search consultant to use these criteria, but you do have to make a conscientious and objective effort to understand, practice, and strengthen them.

Therefore, it is imperative that, after each interview, you immediately sit down and complete the "Interview Assessment Record" found on the next page. Don't wait until the next day to do this. Do it while the interview is still fresh in your mind.

The purpose for most of the areas on this record is self-evident. Review this form now, and then, return to this point and take a look at a few of the best answers you should have checked off upon reviewing your interview. Complete one form after every interview. There is an additional form in Appendix C for you to copy.

Reviewing Your Answers

Look at the line entitled "Description of meeting." The ideal answer is, far and away, hands down, "Dialogue." "Mutual interrogation" is the next best, followed by "Monologue" and "Interrogation." If you checked off anything but "Dialogue" you know that you have to work harder at trying to create a dialogue or conversation approach in your interviews.

Under the "Salary discussion" area, "None" is probably the best answer, followed by "End of meeting." Your answer here indicates whether or not you were successful in establishing your true worth in the employer's eyes before discussing how much it might cost to hire you.

The "First party to state a specific figure" category is simple enough to understand. You are always in a better position if the interviewer states the salary first. This gives you the chance to play your hand in the smartest possible manner.

"Were references requested?" If your answer is yes, you know the employer is interested in you. If your answer is no, don't despair. You could be asked this question at a subsequent interview.

Finally, pay close attention to the "Troublesome questions" section. Be certain to record every question you found yourself having trouble answering. By doing so, you provide yourself with the opportunity to improve upon your answers the next time around.

The Close

You sense the interview drawing to a close. You think it went rather well. If you haven't discussed salary or benefits now might be a good

INTERVIEW ASSESSMENT RECORD

Position _____ Company _____

Interviewer _____ Title _____

Date _____

       ❐ 1st meeting   ❐ 2nd meeting   ❐ 3rd meeting

- Purpose of meeting: ❐ Opening   ❐ Exploratory

- Obtained through: ❐ Cold call   ❐ Recruiter
                      ❐ Response to ad ❐ 3rd party
                      ❐ Broadcast letter ❐ Other

- Length of meeting: _____

- Nature of opening: ❐ None   ❐ New position   ❐ Replacement

- Description of meeting: ❐ Dialogue   ❐ Interrogation
                          ❐ Mutual interrogation ❐ Monologue

- Interviewer rapport: ❐ Excellent   ❐ Good   ❐ Fair   ❐ Poor

- Salary discussion: ❐ None   ❐ Middle of meeting
                    ❐ Early in meeting ❐ End of meeting

- First party to state specific figure:
    ❐ Me   ❐ Interviewer

- Were references requested? ❐ Yes   ❐ No

- Did you obtain information about:

    ❐ Interviewer's background   ❐ Company's structure
    ❐ Company's mode of growth   ❐ Duties of position
    ❐ Location of position   ❐ Your place in flow chart
    ❐ Advancement opportunities ❐ Problems with position
    ❐ Performance evaluation   ❐ What happens next
    ❐ Problems to solve

Troublesome questions: _____

_____

_____

time to bring up the topic. Diplomacy is the key. Perhaps you might introduce the subject by saying something like:

"There's no question in my mind that I could really excel at this position. I know I could quickly contribute to the company's profitability. There's just a few remaining questions I need answered. One is, what kind of money are we talking about?"

Or, you might say:

"I'm extremely interested in this position. There's no doubt in my mind that I could do a great job for you. I guess we've discussed everything about the position except what it pays."

Keep it light, almost inconsequential. Remember, don't bring it up until the close of the interview—if at all. Don't ruin your chances by getting into a confrontation over money. It might serve you well to hold off discussing the salary question until a subsequent interview. If you *do* talk money and the position pays less than you wished for, you might say something to the effect of:

"That's not quite what I hoped it would be. But, I'm still really interested in working for the company."

(Answer and ask)

"Did you say this is a new position? What led to its creation?"

Subsequent Interviews

You probably won't receive an offer at your first interview. If the company is interested, they'll usually ask you back for a subsequent meeting. If the first interview was with personnel, the second one will be with your boss. If the first interview was with your prospective boss, the second interview will probably include staff members and/or the boss's boss.

This second meeting will likely be a straightforward affair, but you might be taken out to dinner and given the opportunity to display your social graces. It should go without saying, do not drink and avoid ordering hard-to-handle dishes such as spaghetti.

Occasionally, an employer will require that final candidates undergo a psychological assessment before being hired. Some companies require candidates to submit a handwriting sample for analysis. If asked to do something like this, the choice is yours—either do it or forget about the company.

Usually you will discover there are two or three other candidates also receiving serious consideration. The best way to prepare for this next go-round is to review the Interview Assessment Record and the notes or tape you made immediately following the prior interview. Dedicate as much time as possible to gathering more information about the company and its products or services. Don't be afraid to write down questions or concerns you have about the position. Take them with you to the next interview.

I'd like to be able to tell you that you will be offered the position at this second meeting, but the chances are good that you won't. This is especially true if you are looking for a management or executive position. Interviews at this level frequently develop into three- or four-meeting affairs strung out over a period of time.

In today's highly competitive, burgeoning job market, it's not unusual to encounter situations that require four or five interviews and sometimes drag on for three to four months. Employers are taking their time and making certain they get the biggest bang for their shrinking buck!

Keep on Looking

Don't stop lining up interviews or interviewing until you have a job. The more offers you can generate the better off you will be. There's no rational explanation, but conducting a job search is often like letting a snowball go down a hill. It was hard work pushing it to the top; but once it's over the top, it gains momentum, and there's no stopping it.

Job search is a numbers game. The more qualified "no's" you get, the closer you get to receiving a "yes." You must generate constant activity to be able to reach the position whereby active interviewing and simultaneous job offers occur. Combine positive morale, persistence, and knowledge and you have the formula for a high octane fuel that can power a job search to undreamed of heights.

Information Interviews

Most job seekers are familiar with information interviewing. Persons with degrees in one area but who, for whatever reason, are trying to break into a different area, should definitely prospect for information interviews.

Unfortunately, too many people have used the information interview as an excuse to get into a company to try to talk their way into a job. For this reason, information interviewing has a bad reputation. If you intend to try to arrange some information interviews, be prepared for an occasionally rude reception.

If the prospective interviewer has the slightest suspicion you're using this as an entry to a possible job opening you will be rebuked, and rightly so. But if you really do need some career advice and direction, by all means go ahead and try it, just be prepared to overcome possible rejection.

Use the telephone technique presented in Chapter 5, "How to Dial Your Way to a Great New Job," to prospect for information interviews. Call the right person and ask if you could possibly get together because you need the advice of an expert in the field. If you can drop a name or two, great!

Example: (After being put through to the right person.)

You:	*Mr. Brown?*
Brown:	*Yes?*
You:	*This is _____. Do you have a minute?*
Brown:	*Yes.*
You:	*Thank you. I've been a _____ with _____ for the past five years. Due to massive cutbacks at _____ I'm in a position to consider making a career change, something I've contemplated for a long time. It seems to me that my background in _____ and my experience in _____ would serve me well in the _____ field. What I really need to do however, is to talk to people such as yourself—people with knowledge and expertise in this field. If you could see your way clear to meet with me for a few minutes I would truly appreciate it. I'm going to be in your area next week. Which day might be best for us to get together?*

Prepare a Notebook

When you do meet with your resource person you must show him or her you are serious about what you're doing; that you're not just another job seeker.

Tell the person you recognize how valuable his time is and you appreciate his meeting with you. Ask the interviewer if he minds if you refer to your notebook so you won't miss asking questions for which you need answers.

Have a separate page for each person with whom you interview. The more pages you have filled out, the more impressed the person will be with your preparation and organization. Jot down the important parts of answers you receive. Maintain as much eye contact as you can.

Each individual's page or pages should have a spot at the top for the usual contact information. Then it should list eight or ten questions with room following each one to record his answers. Copy the information interview forms found at the end of this chapter and in Appendix C if you find the questions meet your needs.

When you do have an information interview, treat it just as you would a job interview. Before you go to the interview, find out all that you can about the company, its products or services, and the person with whom you will be meeting. Be ready to answer all the usual questions. Be prepared to ask intelligent, probing questions concerning the subject matter under discussion.

Try to bring along some "Show and Tell" materials relating to the company, industry, or person you are meeting with. Do some homework. Show the interviewer how organized and efficient you are. Show her you really appreciate her taking the time to meet with you. Make her wish she had more people like you on her staff.

Suppose you are qualified for the position you're investigating. Suppose that you got along with the interviewer and made a good impression. It is possible that you might be considered for employment with the company. In any event, you will have gathered some vital information, engaged in some excellent interviewing experience, and secured a few new names for future leads.

Make Things Happen

All too often, the interview will end with the traditional, "Don't call us, we'll call you" routine. The problem you then face is that of deciding, as objectively as possible, what your chances are of being called back. You could go home, sit by the telephone, and watch for the postal carrier. But the best thing to do is to wait a few days beyond the time stated and then call the interviewer to remind him or her of:

- His or her promise (if he or she promised to call).
- Your impressive qualifications.
- Your burning desire to become part of "the team." Your keen, continued, interest in the position.

For example:

"Hi, Amanda? This is ____(your name)____. I interviewed with you ____(the number of days ago)____ for a ____(the position)____. Do you have a minute? I'm really excited about the possibility of working for you. I know that my experience with _____(insert a SOAR statement)_____ could really benefit the company. However, I wanted to let you know that I do have a couple of other possibilities I'm pursuing. Could you give me some idea as to what my status is?"

In most instances, you will have a pretty good feel for how well the interview went—good, bad, or indifferent. Don't be overcritical of your performance. Don't be too eager to write it off as a lost cause just because you weren't hired the minute you walked in the door.

Have patience. Maintain belief in yourself. If you don't land a position and you believe you've done everything right, you're probably not the right person for the position, nor it for you.

Summary

Whatever your decision, no matter which position you accept, here is a little philosophical offering to keep in mind. As you know, the world of work is rapidly changing. Not too long ago, one was stigmatized as a "job-hopper" if he or she changed companies more than once or twice during a lifetime. *Today, the average American changes companies seven times.* Today, more and more Americans are not only changing jobs and companies but careers.

Given today's job market, it is likely the person doing the interviewing has himself conducted a job search fairly recently. He or she may have transitioned from one industry into another. This is important information to know, particularly if you're seeking to change fields. Not only is there the possibility of discovering and building upon this mutual bridge, but he is certainly in no position to tell you that you can't possibly make such a change.

Employers want to know what you can do for them, not what they can do for you. Sure, they'll ask you what happened on your last job, and, if you were let go, why. But that isn't because they want to hear a sob story. And it certainly isn't because they are anxious to hear you moan and groan and reminisce about the way things used to be. They ask because this is how they judge what you could do for them.

Be positive. Never confess. Never complain. Be specific. Be results oriented. Use SOAR statements. Be alert to what you might do for the employer and for the person interviewing you. Try not to discuss money early in the interview. Ask intelligent and probing questions. Use information you have accumulated. Play "Show and Tell."

Never walk away from an interview not knowing what you can, or cannot, expect to happen next. Don't play the "waiting for the good news by mail game." If the employer is interested in you, he or she will give you a call. Be certain to send a thank-you note. This will place you a step up on virtually all of your competitors.

INFORMATION INTERVIEW FORM—FORM 1

Name _____ Date _____

Title _____

Company _____

Address _____

City _____ State _____ Zip Code _____

How long have you been in this field? _____

_____

_____

_____

What is your background in this field? _____

_____

_____

_____

What does it take to break into or work in this field? _____

_____

_____

_____

What duties and responsibilities go along with the type of position we are

discussing? _____

_____

_____

_____

How important is education versus ability? Experience? _____

_____

_____

_____

INFORMATION INTERVIEW FORM—FORM 2

Name _____ Date _____

What is the most important asset a person should have to be successful in this field? _____

_____

_____

_____

Could I see this job in action? _____

_____

_____

_____

Should I decide to make a career change, how would you recommend I go about making it? _____

_____

_____

_____

What types of positions might I be qualified for in this field? In your company?

_____

_____

_____

Is there another person or company I should talk with? May I use your name?

_____

_____

If you don't mind, I would like to keep you up-to-date concerning my decision.

_____

_____

Chapter 7

How to Minimize Your Efforts and Maximize Results

Your job search will be governed by your personal situation. If you are employed, you will probably not be able to look for work in the same manner and with the same intensity as an unemployed job seeker. Lack of personal funds could also play a part in how you look for work. For example, the telephone is the strongest weapon in your arsenal, but it can be an expensive weapon to use, especially when making out-of-state calls.

Presenting one way to prospect, a way that will accommodate and make the most of each job seeker's personal situation, is an impossibility. If you can afford to, you should use every method detailed in this book. Work smart. Spend your prospecting time proportionately, devoting the most time to those methods promising the best results. Don't permit yourself to fall into the despicable and unproductive habit of doing just those things that are the easiest to do, for example, mailing out three hundred resumes to personnel departments and waiting for a response.

It's your future. The way you work now, looking for work, could determine how, where, and how much you work for the rest of your life. Resolve to be courageous (yes, it takes courage to cold call companies), persistent, and organized. Above all, be prepared for a long haul. That way, if you land a position sooner rather than later, it will be a happy surprise. It was once said that it took one month for every ten thousand dollars of salary to find a new position. That is, if you were making thirty thousand it should take you about three months to find a new job. I would venture to say you can up that one month figure per $10,000 to closer to two months for some positions or industries given today's competitive job market.

One last word of caution: be realistic. Don't price yourself out of a promising position. Keep in mind, the longer you are on the market, the more concerned employers will be about your viability as a candidate. If you have a nice severance package to act as a cushion be particularly concerned about appearing to be someone who can't find a position or really doesn't need to work. So, if the salary offer is close and you like what you have heard and seen, seriously consider the possibility of accepting the offer.

Prospect for opportunity. Land a job with a future. Don't jump out of the frying pan into the fire. The worst thing that could happen to you is to end up back on the street in six months or a year. Then you will *really* have some explaining to do to prospective employers. Find the right job. Establish a track record. Prove yourself and your true worth.

Job Search Central

Set aside a definite area to be job search central. It should be near a phone. Keep all of your records, correspondence, and books here. Your typewriter or computer, resumes, letterhead, and envelopes should be here also. Make this your private domain. Post a "Private! Keep Out! Great Mind at Work!" sign if necessary.

Taking Calls

Tell everyone who might answer your phone exactly what you would like them to say. Make sure they take down every message accurately, including the date and time of the call. Use an answering machine when no one is there to take calls. Keep your recorded message brief and businesslike. This is not the time to show off your great Elvis impersonation! Sound professional, friendly, and enthusiastic.

Staying Organized

Keep this area neat. Pick up and organize every day. Consider your job search your new job and job search central your office. Report to work on time, every day, five days a week. Get dressed up if it helps you work better. Plan your work and work your plan.

Record Keeping

Lead Book

Purchase a three-ring binder. Label it "Leads." Fill it with lead sheets like those "starters" provided at the conclusion of this chapter and in Appendix C. Each lead sheet in your lead book will contain pertinent information about a contact you have made. Keep it current.

Use a new page for each lead. Print the company's name, the relative's name, and so on, at the top of each page in the appropriate space. Keep the pages in alphabetical order by name. When you have a large number of leads, buy some alphabetized divider tabs to facilitate the use of this book. If you need to record more information than the front of the page allows, turn the page over and continue writing or simply three-hole punch an 8½″ by 11″ sheet of paper and add it to the book.

Photocopy the Lead Sheet form at the end of this chapter to make the number of lead sheets you need. Three-hole punch these copies and place them in your lead book. Use your lead book to record *all* contacts. When recording information about an ad, tape the ad right to the front of the lead sheet for that company. Any time you send a cover letter to a company, turn that company's lead sheet over and copy the cover letter on the back side.

The Necessity of Keeping Complete Records

It is imperative you keep your lead book as detailed and as up-to-date as possible. If you conduct an energetic, all-out job search, it will very soon start to fill up with pages of leads. Then, one day you will receive a call from a person or company you forgot all about. Unless your lead book is up-to-date and organized, it could prove to be very embarrassing. Because you have maintained your records efficiently you will have no problem. You will ask the employer:

> *"Could you please hold the line for just a few seconds? I'll be right back. Thank you."*

You run to your lead book. As you head back to the phone with the book in your hands, you flip through the alphabetized pages to that company's name. You quickly review the information there, pick up the receiver, and with enthusiasm and a businesslike tone you say:

> *"Thank you for waiting Ms. Oliver. I'm really happy you called. I'm still interested in the position we talked about two months ago."*

Another reason for thorough record keeping? To systematically review and reconnect each lead seven times, pursuing it to its bitter or victorious end. (See "Networking and the Rule of Seven," in Chapter 4 "How to Develop, Contact, and Pursue Job Leads.")

Activities Calendar

An activities calendar is used to remind yourself of things to do: calls to be made on certain days at certain times, interview days and times, contacts to be made, materials, books, and articles to be read. Don't forget to include dates, times, and locations of association meetings, conventions, exhibits, job fairs, and similar networking activities. Your activities calendar should note when a resume has been mailed as well as when to recontact the company if no reply is forthcoming by a certain date. Before you take the action called for, be certain to review or have on hand the appropriate page of information found in your lead book.

Consult your calendar the last thing each day and the first thing when you begin prospecting the next day. Use a calendar with a big block of space for each day, so you will have plenty of room to record the history of your search. An activities calendar provides a visible, albeit sometimes painful, reminder of the effectiveness or ineffectiveness of your search efforts. Empty blocks of space are symptomatic of an unhealthy job search.

A typical activities calendar entry:

10

8–9 A.M.	Cold calls to Association list
9 A.M.–noon	Library research
Noon	Lunch with Rick
2 P.M.	Interview—Jane Whistler at TJM
5 P.M.	Phone John James at Apex Corp.
7 P.M.	Professionals Assn. Meeting

Resumes mailed to Judy Finn and Robert Roth.

Set Goals

A job seeker without realistic, attainable goals is like a ship without a rudder. Determine your own goals based upon the amount of time you can realistically devote to your search. Once these goals are determined and prove attainable, *meet them.* Let nothing stand in your way.

You will find a Weekly Job Search Evaluation form and scoring system on the next few pages. There is an additional evaluation form in Appendix C. Complete a new form at the conclusion of each week of your search. Refer to it and update it daily. If you find the 125-point weekly total to be less than challenging, increase your point goal for the upcoming week to perhaps 150 points. Be certain whatever point total you set for yourself is realistically attainable.

What are some realistic goals? Start with the Rule of Seven. If you have twenty people in your network, call ten per week every two weeks until you have made seven calls to each contact in a fourteen week period of time. That's just two calls to two different contacts each day. Of course you can't know how many ads you are going to happen upon, but naturally you are going to answer all of them. Employment agencies? At least five to ten if possible. Call them every two weeks also. How many cold calls to companies should you make each day? Instead of calling a certain number per day, try this—make as many calls as it takes each day to actually talk to two or three bosses.

A Good Time to Call

Usually, the best time to contact prospective employers is early in the morning, as early as 8:00 A.M. Another good time to contact bosses is at lunch or right after everyone else has gone home at the end of the work day. Let the phone ring a little longer than you normally would. The boss himself might answer his phone.

Keep Trying

Always follow up on all leads and do not give up until they tell you to get lost. If you are prospecting for a sales job you should hang in there until they threaten to have you arrested for harassment.

Call Back

If you lost out on a job call back in two or three weeks, "Just to see if the person that did get it is working out." Maybe that person *didn't* work out, or perhaps another job has opened up in the meanwhile. Persistence is the one commodity job seekers can never have enough of. Like so much of life, job hunting is quite often a case of being in the right place at the right time. Some might call it luck; but, in this case, luck is what happens when preparation meets opportunity.

Time Management

Study the activities shown on the Weekly Job Search Evaluation sheet. Use it to prioritize your efforts and to objectively measure your search progress on a weekly basis. This will remind you of what you must do to be successful. How much time should you devote to your campaign? There are varying opinions on this subject. But if you spend four or five hours a day conscientiously covering all the bases as recommended, you deserve the rest of the day off.

Weekly Job Search Evaluation—Scoring System

Interview with Probable Boss—25 points. This is the highest possible score you may award yourself for any singular search activity. The reason for this being the highest possible score is obvious—no meeting with a prospective or probable boss, no job.

Interview with Personnel—15 points. In many instances, meeting with personnel is a key link in the hiring chain. Rarely, especially at the salaried level, does personnel do the actual hiring. But, when you manage to win an interview with personnel, you have taken a big step in the right direction.

Recontact with Probable Boss—12 points. When you recontact a probable boss you are keeping your chances alive by maintaining a high profile. Often when you recontact this hiring authority you are able to cite more reasons why he should seriously consider your candidacy, further strengthening your candidacy. Additionally, you show the employer that you are seriously interested in working for the company and have the initiative to do what it takes to land the job.

In-Person Interview with Network Contact—10 points. In-person, face-to-face get-togethers provide the opportunity to make things happen, to get to know and like one another. Whether it's a network contact, a recruiter, or a probable boss, getting liked can be terribly important to your future relationship. Telephone or mail contact is very limiting and impersonal.

In-Person Interview with Recruiter—10 points. The same reasoning prevails. When someone knows and likes you, likes the way you carry yourself, likes what you have to sell, he or she will work harder to be of assistance. In the recruiter's case, he or she will feel more confident sending you on interviews.

Telephone Contact with Probable Boss—8 points

Telephone Interview with Network Contact or Recruiter—6 points

Letter or Resume to Probable Boss—6 points

Recontact with Personnel—5 points

Telephone Interview with Personnel—5 points

The rest of the scores range from 4 points down to 1 point. Your objective? *Accumulate at least 125 points per week.*

WEEKLY JOB SEARCH EVALUATION

Week of _____

		Value	Contacts	Total
"Cold" contacts				
Resume and/or letter to ...	*Network contact*	2	____	____
	Recruiter	2	____	____
	Personnel	1	____	____
	Probable boss	2	____	____
Response to ad				
Resume and/or letter to ...	*Recruiter*	3	____	____
	Personnel	3	____	____
	Probable boss	6	____	____
"Cold" calls				
Telephone contact with ...	*Network contact*	4	____	____
	Recruiter	4	____	____
	Personnel	3	____	____
	Probable boss	8	____	____
Interviews				
Telephone interview with ...	*Network contact*	6	____	____
	Recruiter	6	____	____
	Personnel	5	____	____
	Probable boss	10	____	____
In-person interview with ...	*Network contact*	10	____	____
	Recruiter	10	____	____
	Personnel	15	____	____
	Probable boss	25	____	____
Re-contacts with ...				
	Network contact	2	____	____
	Recruiter	3	____	____
	Personnel	5	____	____
	Probable boss	12	____	____

Observations and Comments

Multiply the value of the activity by the number of contacts recorded under the Contacts column heading. Add all of the totals under the Total column heading to determine your weekly point total. Using this scoring system and striving to meet the 125 points per week figure will lead you to do those activities that score the highest number of points. Your greatest chances of success also lie in performing these activities.

Avoid Burnout

Experience indicates, job hunters who pull out all the stops and go at it full tilt for a week or so soon suffer burnout. Not only this, but it takes time for many job search activities to begin to take root. You cannot, nor should not, expect immediate success.

Plan on your campaign taking a minimum of three months. The higher up the corporate ladder you are, the longer it normally takes to obtain the job you want. Someone earning about sixty thousand can expect to take up to eight months or so, given today's job market. If you land the job you want sooner than that, wonderful. If not, keep at it.

Work at conducting the most intelligent, well organized, energized campaign you possibly can. Not only will it serve you well right here and now, but it will set a standard for any campaigns you might conduct in the future. You can never tell when you might have to, or decide to, prospect for work. Paying your dues now can reap big dividends in the future, as well as in the present.

Don't neglect your family or social life while on the job hunt. Set aside time to do many, if not all, the things you like to do. When you work diligently at your new job of looking for a new job, you deserve some rewards. So does your family.

There's no avoiding it, no matter how enthused and organized you are, conducting a job search can provide many anxious and depressing moments. Those around you will not only share your anxiety and lows, but they will have concerns of their own generated by this temporary condition. Stop to appreciate the anxiety they are experiencing. Be thoughtful. It's tough enough looking for work without arousing any unnecessary, thoughtless, turmoil.

You will find the "10 Strategies for Job Search Success" in Appendix A. Refer to them often during your campaign. If you find yourself spinning your wheels, these strategies will get your job search back on track.

Conclusion

Knowledge is power waiting to be activated. You now possess this knowledge. You are truly the master of your own destiny. Use what you have learned to reach out and seize your future today. Remember, the ten most powerful two-letter words in the English language are:

IF IT IS TO BE, IT IS UP TO ME!

LEAD SHEET

Company: _____

Name: _____ Phone: _____

Contact: _____

Title: _____ Secretary: _____

Address: _____

_____

Contact Date: _____

Result:

Contact Date: _____

Result:

Contact Date: _____

Result:

Appendix A

10 Strategies for Job Search Success

1. Never Reject Yourself

If you believe you have most of the qualifications called for in a job—
go for it! Nothing happens in a job search until you sit down to talk
with people. Let others reject you, don't do it to yourself. Reject
yourself, and you'll end up talking to yourself on the unemployment
line. Here are a few of the things that might happen when you land
an interview despite reservations about your qualifications:

- You might be offered another more suitable position.
- You might be given the training required to do the job.
- You might have an opening created for you to take advantage
  of your particular talents or experience.
- You might be kept in mind for future openings.
- You might be directed to another more suitable company.
- You might even be offered the job.

Wonderful things can happen, if you *never reject yourself.*

2. If it Sells, Use it. If it Doesn't, Don't

However you communicate with an employer—in person, in writing, over the phone—reveal only your saleable assets. It's amazing how many job seekers fail to follow this advice. This is especially true when it comes to writing a resume.

If you think you're too old for the job, don't include your age. If you feel you're overqualified, downplay your achievements and experience. If you are in less than perfect health, don't talk about it. There are no state or federal laws governing what has to go into a resume. Be honest, but don't be a fool and self-destruct.

When you are buying a car does the salesperson dwell on its bad points? You are now a salesperson no matter what type of position you are seeking. Increase your chances for sales success; if it *sells, use it. If it doesn't, don't.*

3. Never Mail Your Resume Unless You Have to

Mailing your resume to an employer makes being rejected too easy. The best thing to do is to call on the phone, get the boss's name and try to arrange a get-together. (Don't even call it an interview.) Avoid such rejection-inviting statements as "I'm looking for a job" and "I was wondering, do you happen to have any openings?" Elevate yourself above the job-hunting crowd.

If you can, drop a name or say something nice about the company and its product or service. Then, launch right into your sales pitch. Give two or three of your strongest and most pertinent sales points. Back up each of these points with a specific example to validate it.

After you have whet the listener's appetite go for the get-together. Say that you would like to stop by, get to meet him or her and drop off your resume. Say that it will only take a minute or two. Tell him, "Name the day and the time, and I'll be there."

Is the employer located too far away? Can't reach him by phone? Too timid to try? Mail your resume, wait five or six days, and then call. But your best course of action is to *never mail your resume unless you have to.*

4. Always Contact the Person You Would Report to

Don't contact the person or department listed in an ad. Go higher up the corporate ladder, especially in large companies. Contact the person who would be your boss. This person best knows the personnel needs of the department and will most likely do the hiring. How can you find out who this person is? Call the company and ask:

> "Could you tell me the name of the person in charge of (your area)?" Or, "Who would your _____(your area)_____ people report to?" And, when told the name, continue with . . . "How do you spell _____(boss's name)_____? Is that Dr., Mr., Miss, Mrs., or Ms., _____(name)_____? What is _____(name)_____ 's correct job title?" Record all of this information on a job search lead sheet. Then ask, "Could I speak with _____(name)_____ please?"

When you encounter a secretary, be polite and treat her with respect. If she offers to help, let her. Ask for her name and use it. "Thank you _____(her name)_____. Perhaps you might suggest the best time for me to call back?"*Always contact the person you would report to.*

5. Don't Ask "No" Questions

Once you have reached this person, you should present yourself as positively as possible. Keep your sales pitch brief. Avoid asking such questions as: "Do you have any openings?" or "Can I drop by with my resume and talk with you?"

The problem with questions presented in this manner is that they automatically provoke a negative response from the listener. Phrase your questions so that it is virtually impossible to answer them with an automatic "no." "I'll be in your area next Monday and Tuesday. Which day might be best for us to meet?" *Don't ask "no" questions.*

6. Prospect for Interviews—Not Openings

Don't wait for the Sunday help-wanted ads to look for work. That's what everyone does. Work harder *and smarter* than your competition. Call or, when forced to, write every company that might hire a person with your credentials. Contact companies whether or not you know they have openings.

If you call and receive the "sorry, no openings" line, just say cheerfully, "That's all right. I didn't expect you would have an opening. However, when something does open up, I want to be the first one you call."

Then press on without delay. Get the interview. "I'd like to stop by, drop off my resume, and get to meet you. It will only take a minute or two. You name the time, and I'll be there."

Of course, you are not going to ignore the help-wanted ads. But, you uncover jobs your competition will never see in any ad when you *prospect for interviews, not openings.*

7. Always Use an Old Lead to Develop a New Lead

The most depressing day in a job seeker's life is when the lead bank runs dry. You *must* replenish the leads you withdraw. One of the quickest and easiest ways to do this is to ask an old lead to give you a new lead. Don't ask necessarily to be told of a job opening, but rather for the name of some company or person who might be able to help you in any way. If the old lead is willing to call and arrange a get-together, great! If not, ask if you can use his or her name when you call. Avoid job hunting bankruptcy. *Always use an old lead to develop a new lead.*

8. Use Every Possible Resource

You cannot gain a competitive edge if you limit your job search activities to answering help-wanted ads. Most jobs are unadvertised and are filled by word-of-mouth. Contact friends, relatives, and social acquaintances. Contact past workmates, your doctor, and even your family insurance agent. Contact anybody and everybody you know. Tell them you are looking for a job. Continue to touch base with these people about once every two weeks for at least seven times each.

Use reputable employment agencies or executive search firms. Some agencies will limit search activities to specialized fields such as engineering, medical, and clerical. Other agencies will work with employees in general. When qualified, use both types. Never pay anybody. Use your network. Use directories, newspapers, and trade journals. Network, network, network. *Use every possible resource.*

9. Never Confess. Never Complain

When interviewing, always try to picture yourself in the interviewer's place. If you were conducting the interview what kinds of answers would you like to hear? What questions could a job seeker ask you that might impress you?

Do your homework before the interview. How big is the company? How many locations does it have? What does it manufacture, service, and sell? How long has it been in business? How much money did it make (or lose) last year?

Be positive. Because you have done your homework you will be able to answer and ask questions intelligently. Keep the dialogue upbeat. Don't allow the interviewer to flush out your weaknesses, pet peeves, or how you *really* felt, or feel, about a past boss, employer, or situation.

Over the long haul, day in and day out, we all like to work with hard-working, conscientious, friendly people. No one likes to work with a moaner and groaner—no matter how brilliant he or she may be. *Never confess. Never complain.*

10. Always Send a Thank-You Note

Have you ever received an unexpected thank-you note? How did it make you feel? How did you feel about the person who took the time to write it? If that person ever needed your help would you refuse it?

When you get home from an interview, sit down and immediately write a thank-you note to your interviewer. Then pop it into the next mail.

Very few job seekers take the time to write even the briefest thank-you note following an interview. It might be all that it takes to tip the scales in your favor. And, even if you don't get this particular job, the employer could very easily give you another good lead or two should you ask—as you should.

Besides saying "thank you," make sure you use this occasion to once again sell yourself. Review the interview in your mind. Try to think of a few points that seemed to be important and address these points. Once again tell the interviewer what you can do for both the department and the company.

Type the note if you can. If you have good penmanship, write it out in longhand. But, above all, *always send a thank-you note.*

Appendix B
52 Tips That Can Make a Job Hunter's Year

#1

Don't ask "no" questions. Don't ask questions that can be answered with a "no." Ask instead, "Which would be best . . . ?" "What do you do . . . ?" Whenever you receive a no for an answer, just remember, you asked for it.

#2

Want to learn a prospective boss's name? Use the mailing list routine. Call the company and say, "I'm updating my mailing list. Are you still at 2323 Armstrong? Is your zip still 23456? And your Vice President of Manufacturing is?"

#3

Don't expect your network contacts to remember you if you only contact them once or twice. Out of sight, out of mind. Use the salesperson's Rule of Seven. If they haven't helped you after seven contacts, move on to greener pastures.

#4

What have you done to better yourself? Nothing? Bring along a course catalog from a local college to your interview. Highlight a few courses. When asked this question, immediately ask the interviewer if he has a minute. Take out the catalog and open it to the highlighted page. Ask if the interviewer would be kind enough to recommend which of the highlighted courses you should investigate.

#5

Never leave an interview without knowing what will happen next. Thank the interviewer for the interview. If you want the job tell him or her so. Recap a few of your strongest qualifications. Then ask, "Where do we go from here?"

#6

When dealing with secretaries, use the Secretary's Rule; treat her with respect and make a friend. Don't try to end-run, steamroll, or "honey" her to death. The best way to make her a friend? Ask and use her name. Thank her for her assistance. *A caution:* use her name two or three times but don't beat her over the head with it.

#7

When asked if the boss may call you back, say, "I'm going to be away from my desk off and on today. Perhaps you would be kind enough to suggest a good time for me to call back?" You always want to be in the proper job search mind-set when dealing with employers. Don't be caught off guard. Better to catch *them* off guard.

#8

Never tell an interviewer how great you are without backing it up. Example: "I'm a really dependable employee. In the last three years I only missed three days due to illness. When you hire me you can expect me to be there to do the job and to do it right." Or, "I have extensive experience in labor negotiations. Let me tell you about one potentially explosive situation I almost single-handedly helped to diffuse."

#9

Did you place second in the hiring process? If, after a few weeks, you're still unemployed, call the interviewer. Tell her you are still interested in working for the company. And, you're calling on the chance that "things didn't work out" with the candidate they selected. This could be all it takes to spark renewed interest in you. Maybe the selected candidate *didn't* pan out. Maybe they have a new opening.

#10

After receiving help from a secretary whom you don't know say "Thank you, I appreciate that. Who am I speaking with please?" Then, immediately call her by name, "Well, Nancy . . ." When closing out the conversation, use her name again, casually. "Thanks, Nancy, I'll call back tomorrow as you suggested." Guess what the first word out of your mouth is when you call back and she answers?

#11

The interview doesn't end when you walk out of the employer's office. The first chance you have, sit down and write your interviewer a short thank-you note. It's a thoughtful gesture, one that the great majority of your competitors will fail to make. This is yet another way to elevate yourself above the masses and it only takes a few minutes. Be sure to include a sales point or two.

#12

Resume doesn't fit the position you are interested in? Write a one-page LetteRes. Highlight those qualifications you have that *do* fit the job description. If they are specific, quantified accomplishments all the better. A LetteRes is simply a mini-resume disguised as a cover letter. Because it is one page it will get read. If the reader likes what he or she reads you will be called for more information.

#13

Use the SOAR formula when describing your accomplishment. First, state the Subject, followed by an Overview of the situation, followed by the Action you took, and, of course, the Results of this action. Keep it brief. Be specific. Cite quantifiers: dollars, numbers, and percentages. Use a single SOAR statement per accomplishment. Each statement should take no longer than a minute to relate.

#14

Aren't quite sure of how to dress for an interview? Call the employer and ask. For example: "I have an interview coming up next week in your accounting department. If you could tell me how the women in that department dress, I would really appreciate it."

#15

Use quantifiers whenever possible when citing an accomplishment, duty, or responsibility. Dollars. Numbers. Percentages. If you think the number may be overkill, downplay it a little. The way you state such a figure might well vary depending upon the size of the employer. For example: you might want to be somewhat more modest when talking with a small sized company. However, never, never, never make up a number just to sound impressive. If you can't come up with an honest approximation, don't use a quantifier.

#16

Here are three great ways to remind a network contact that you need his help. 1. Send him a highlighted copy of a newspaper or magazine article you think will interest him. 2. Call. Should a secretary tell you that he's unavailable, ask her to tell him you called "just to touch base." 3. Call to ask him out to lunch. Even if he can't make it, it will keep your name in his mind.

#17

When your experience matches the job qualifications almost to a tee, consider writing a two-column cover letter. After the introductory paragraph, write the job qualifications called for under one column titled "Requirements." Show specifically how well you meet each of these qualifications under an adjacent column titled "Qualifications." If there is a particular qualification you don't meet, leave it out or replace it with one you think should impress the reader.

#18

Upon arriving at the interviewer's office, ask the secretary or receptionist where there is a rest room you might use to "freshen up." Make sure your tie is on straight, no dandruff on the collar, hair in place, etc. And smile. Take a look around. If the room is empty, say aloud to the image in the mirror, "You handsome devil you. This company is sure lucky you've taken an interest in it."

#19

Eliminate "weasel" words from your job hunting vocabulary. Never say "I think . . ." when you can say, "I know . . . ." Never say, "I believe . . ." when you can say, "there isn't a doubt in my mind." Never say, "I feel . . ." when you could say, "it is . . ." or, "it definitely is . . . ."

#20

When interviewing, use letters of recommendation, as well as a list of references. With letters, you know exactly what someone is saying about you. Don't like what's being said? Discard it. When requested during an interview, letters of reference can immediately add to your stature and saleability. They might also shorten the interview process. The employer doesn't have to chase down your references.

#21

Don't use "Dear Sir or Madam" or "To Whom It May Concern" when mailing a resume to an unknown party. Use the usual cover letter form: date, title of prospective boss, company, street, state, and zip code. Then, skip three or four lines and launch right into the introductory paragraph of the letter. How do you feel about getting mail that uses such "endearing" salutations? Employers are people like you. They feel the same way.

#22

Play "Show and Tell" for big kids at your interviews. Collect and share copies of annual reports, samples of work (if possible), sales material showing product information, and what you worked with or on. Example: If you are in manufacturing, you might obtain a sales brochure that shows what the employer manufactured or the type of machinery and equipment it used.

#23

Afraid of pricing yourself out of a possible job offer? State just your base salary. Then, after the employer is really interested in you, you can attempt to add benefits and perks to sweeten the pot: a company car, expenses, stock options, association memberships, paid vacations, etc. To do so too early in the hiring process might result in shooting yourself in the foot.

#24

Need to find out what company placed a post office box ad? Call the post office and ask. They should tell you. If questioned as to why you want to know, you might say, "I'm collecting unemployment. If I am to continue to collect it, I have to let the employment office know the companies I prospect with each week." Usually, this is all it takes for a reluctant postal worker to reveal the employer's name.

#25

Do not limit your networking to your immediate circle of friends, relatives, and business associates. There's a phenomenon associated with networking known as The Strength of Weak Ties. Simply stated, The Strength of Weak Ties states that, it's the people you have never met who are most likely to be of assistance in your job search. Remember that old rhyme, "Make new friends and keep the old, one is silver and the other gold."

#26

Another reason to arrive at your interviewer's office just a few minutes early. You might be asked to fill out an application. This becomes the interviewer's guide for the journey ahead. Better for you, if your journey follows your road map, your resume. Hopefully, the interview will begin on time. By being just a few minutes early, the interviewer may forgo having you complete the application before the interview.

#27

Answer and ask. When responding to an interviewer's questions follow your answer with an appropriate, related question. Question: "What has been your greatest accomplishment?" Answer the question and then ask: "Is that the type of thing that would help me to accomplish this job?" Being interrogated serves no worthwhile purpose for you or for the employer. To be successful, interviews must be mutually beneficial.

#28

Answering the money question. It is essential you understand the philosophy behind answering the money question, especially since the question may occur early on in an interview. The basic reason you do not want to answer the money question at this time is this: when you have a successful interview, you will always be worth more in the interviewer's eyes at the end than at the beginning.

#29

Don't hesitate to ask your interviewer questions. Should you be offered the position, you will need information upon which to make an intelligent decision. Example: an employer asks, "Tell me about your last boss." After responding in as positive a fashion as possible you ask, "I guess this would be a good time to ask you if you would be my boss?" Perhaps followed by, "Would you mind telling me how long you have been with the company?" Two weeks? It's a whole new ballgame.

#30

If asked how much you are looking for early on in an interview, you might respond, "That's an important question. But I really don't know enough about the position to give you a good answer." Now, ask a question or questions to lead the interviewer away from the question just asked. Examples: "Could you tell me why this position is available?"

#31

If an employer insists that he wants "an answer" right then and there, watch out. Why is he so anxious? Is it a hard-to-fill, short-lived position? Is he afraid that should you get to know him better you might not want to work for him? Whatever the reason, put off answering if you can. If you really need the income and he presses you, say yes. You can always give your notice should something better come along.

#32

Review your daily job search activities to see if you set and met realistic yet challenging goals. Don't measure your success in calling employers by the number of them you called. Just calling means little or nothing. Measure your progress by the number of decision makers with whom you actually conversed.

#33

Monday is a great day for answering ads, mailing broadcast letters, conducting record maintenance, and researching employers. There is usually too much activity on a Monday in companies to enable you to experience any degree of contact success. Friday is another day to avoid, especially after lunch. You can find enough other things to do on these two days to keep yourself productively busy.

#34

Seriously consider sending your interviewer a "tent style" thank-you note immediately following an interview. You can buy some very nice, business-like ones in any good card shop. If the note is off-white all the better. You want it to stand out on the interviewer's desk. A tent style note makes it easier to find enough sales oriented things to say than if you tried to fill a standard 8½″ × 11″ sheet of stationery.

#35

Can't find out anything about the employer you will be interviewing with? Between reference materials and network contacts, this shouldn't be. However, if you have to, you can always call and ask lightheartedly, "Help. I have an interview coming up over there in a few days and I can't find out a darn thing about what you guys do. I don't want to make a fool of myself. Are you a branch of the CIA or what?"

#36

Never take a position without finding out why it is open. If you have to, continue to probe and ask questions until you are satisfied that you have an accurate idea of what actually transpired. Other good questions to ask? How long has this position been open? Is there a problem with this position? What happened to the person who held it? The answers to any or all of these questions could prove to be real eye-openers.

#37

Never confess, never complain. If you can't find something good to say about someone or something, don't say anything. The noise you occasionally hear in an interview is that of corporate "rats," dissatisfied employees, deep down in the galleys of the corporate ship of state, feverishly gnawing away at the timbers. Employers are blessed with enough moaners and groaners. They aren't looking to add another "rat" to the pack.

#38

You are often asked about people you have worked for. If you, like some of us, have that certain someone, "following you around," here's a way to phrase an answer to such a question. "If you really want to know what my last boss would have to say about me you'd have to ask her. Naturally, I can't speak for her or anyone else. Hopefully, she would tell you that . . ." Now, do not stop, go, launch immediately into one of your best sales points.

#39

Don't believe everything an interviewer tells you to be true. He may really believe what he is telling you to be true, when it really isn't. Example: you ask about the person's management style and he replies, "I believe in a management team concept. We all have to work together if we expect to score." If you're smart, you will follow up answers such as this with, "That's great. Approximately how often do you have team meetings?" And, "What transpires at these meetings."

#40

Always ask an interviewer what problems are associated with the position. When he tells you, you can direct your attention to showing the person how you can help to solve those problems. Or, you may decide, there's no way I want to become involved in this problem! Problem solvers get hired. No problems? Stand up. Shake the interviewer's hand. Say as you head for the door, "I've always wanted to go to heaven but I'm still a little too young to make the move."

#41

Dead duck intros. If you find yourself prefacing your answers with phrases such as "To tell you the truth . . ." "Between you and me . . ." and "Frankly, I . . ." watch out! You are about to become a dead duck. No matter how comfortable you are with an interviewer, do not confess, complain, or admit. It's a guaranteed way of getting shot down. It's the interviewers you really like who can get all the information they need out of you. Stay on your guard.

#42

Do hobbies and interests belong on a resume? Perhaps—if you have the room, and if what you have to say will arouse the interviewer's interest. Consider how many people play golf, tennis, ski, etc. If your interest matches that of your interviewer, you are on the way to breaking down barriers. Also, uncommon hobbies such as slot car racing and scuba diving can often lead to lively, barrier breaking, discussions.

#43

Another way to try to avoid answering the money question too early in the interview: When asked, you respond, "Don't misunderstand me, money is important (you're not about to "give" yourself away), but it's not my number one priority. I've been around long enough to know that how my boss and I get along can mean the difference between success and failure. Would you be my boss?" Without this immediate follow-up question, he or she will go right back to the original one and you'll be forced to answer.

#44

Can't get through to the decision maker? Try calling before or after normal working hours. Let the phone ring. He might find it difficult to ignore. Another good time? Try lunch. He may be minding his own phone if his secretary is out to lunch. You might even try on a Saturday morning in the event he came into the office to catch up on his work.

#45

Before accepting an offer, be certain to learn what the future may hold. Can you be promoted? To what? Who decides? What are the criteria for advancement? How often will you be evaluated? Is it written or oral? What if you disagree with the evaluation? Do you have recourse? When told a reasonable "trial" period before being offered the chance to move up, always remind the interviewer that you will remind him of it. Then, a few months before that period is up, gently remind him of his words.

#46

When cold calling employers, bosses or their secretaries, begin your conversation with, "This is Martin Mulberry from Standard Republic. That last name's spelled M-u-l-b-e-r-r-y. I'd like to speak with Mr. Big please." When you spell your name, the listener will put aside what he or she may be doing to listen. Names, companies' and people's, play a vital role in opening doors. Use them whenever possible.

#47

Tell me about yourself. Avoid answering this common opening request in the same way as your competitors. Forget telling where you graduated from college, your degree, you first position, etc. Instead, launch right into a major, validated and quantified accomplishment. After spending no more than a minute on your answer, conclude with a question such as, "Is this the type of information you're looking for?" Make your first punch a knock-out one.

#48

Never reject yourself. Want the position? Think you can do it? Go for it! Even if you're not right for this position, the interviewer might: have another more suitable position, know of another such position within the company, create a position to take advantage of your experience, give you the name of a person or company that would be interested in you. You'll suffer enough rejection in the days ahead. Why do it to yourself?

#49

Prospect for interviews, not openings. Of course you will respond to openings you hear of. However, by prospecting for a "get-together," you give the employer no reason to head you off at the pass with the "no opening" line. Getting hired means sitting down face-to-face with the decision maker. Tell the employer you would like to drop by with your resume and chat with him or her for just a minute or two. If something should open up, knowing about you could save him or her a lot of time and money.

#50

Always use an old lead to develop a new lead. Leads are like money in the bank. Spend them all and one day you'll wake up flat broke. This is far and away one of the most depressing things to happen to a job seeker. Every contact you make, you must make it a point to ask for additional names of companies and people for you to contact. Don't worry whether or not you or your contacts think their contacts will have a job for you. Just get all the names you can and continue to make them multiply.

#51

Never mail your resume if you can avoid it. Contact the decision maker by phone. Go for a short "get-together." 100 percent of your competition will be mailing out resumes, mostly to personnel. Very few of your competitors will mail their resume to the hiring authority and then follow up with a phone call. Rise above the masses. End run the rest of the field. Call, get the meeting, hand your resume to the decision maker when you meet him or her for the first time.

#52

Commit these words to memory. Post them where you can see them every day as you begin and end your search activities. They are the ten most important two-letter words in the English language. They're wonderful words to live by, but job seekers in particular should pay them great heed. "IF IT IS TO BE, IT IS UP TO ME."

Appendix C
Job Search Forms

(Make copies of the following forms and keep a record of each and every one of your contacts.)

INTERVIEW ASSESSMENT RECORD

Position _____ Company _____

Interviewer _____ Title _____

Date _____

☐ 1st meeting   ☐ 2nd meeting   ☐ 3rd meeting

• Purpose of meeting: ☐ Opening   ☐ Exploratory

• Obtained through: ☐ Cold call   ☐ Recruiter
                          ☐ Response to ad   ☐ 3rd party
                          ☐ Broadcast letter ☐ Other

• Length of meeting: _____

• Nature of opening: ☐ None   ☐ New position   ☐ Replacement

• Description of meeting: ☐ Dialogue   ☐ Interrogation
                            ☐ Mutual interrogation ☐ Monologue

• Interviewer rapport: ☐ Excellent   ☐ Good   ☐ Fair   ☐ Poor

• Salary discussion: ☐ None   ☐ Middle of meeting
                           ☐ Early in meeting ☐ End of meeting

• First party to state specific figure:
      ☐ Me   ☐ Interviewer

• Were references requested?   ☐ Yes   ☐ No

• Did you obtain information about:

      ☐ Interviewer's background   ☐ Company's structure
      ☐ Company's mode of growth   ☐ Duties of position
      ☐ Location of position   ☐ Your place in flow chart
      ☐ Advancement opportunities   ☐ Problems with position
      ☐ Performance evaluation   ☐ What happens next
      ☐ Problems to solve

Troublesome questions: _____

_____

_____

INFORMATION INTERVIEW FORM—FORM 1

Name _____ Date _____

Title _____

Company _____

Address _____

City _____ State_____ Zip Code _____

How long have you been in this field? _____

_____

_____

_____

What is your background in this field? _____

_____

_____

_____

What does it take to break into or work in this field? _____

_____

_____

_____

What duties and responsibilities go along with the type of position we are

discussing? _____

_____

_____

_____

How important is education versus ability? Experience? _____

_____

_____

_____

INFORMATION INTERVIEW FORM—FORM 2

Name _____ Date _____

What is the most important asset a person should have to be successful in this field? _____

_____

_____

_____

Could I see this job in action? _____

_____

_____

_____

Should I decide to make a career change, how would you recommend I go about making it? _____

_____

_____

_____

What types of positions might I be qualified for in this field? In your company?

_____

_____

_____

Is there another person or company I should talk with? May I use your name?

_____

_____

If you don't mind, I would like to keep you up-to-date concerning my decision.

_____

_____

LEAD SHEET

Company: _____

Name: _____ Phone: _____

Contact: _____

Title: _____ Secretary: _____

Address: _____

_____

Contact Date: _____

Result:

Contact Date: _____

Result:

Contact Date: _____

Result:

WEEKLY JOB SEARCH EVALUATION

Week of _____

		Value	Contacts	Total
"Cold" contacts				
Resume and/or letter to ...	*Network contact*	2	____	____
	Recruiter	2	____	____
	Personnel	1	____	____
	Probable boss	2	____	____
Response to ad				
Resume and/or letter to ...	*Recruiter*	3	____	____
	Personnel	3	____	____
	Probable boss	6	____	____
"Cold" calls				
Telephone contact with ...	*Network contact*	4	____	____
	Recruiter	4	____	____
	Personnel	3	____	____
	Probable boss	8	____	____
Interviews				
Telephone interview with ...	*Network contact*	6	____	____
	Recruiter	6	____	____
	Personnel	5	____	____
	Probable boss	10	____	____
In-person interview with ...	*Network contact*	10	____	____
	Recruiter	10	____	____
	Personnel	15	____	____
	Probable boss	25	____	____
Re-contacts with ...				
	Network contact	2	____	____
	Recruiter	3	____	____
	Personnel	5	____	____
	Probable boss	12	____	____

Observations and Comments

Appendix D
Newspaper Index

Contact Information for a Major Newspaper in Each of the Fifty States and in Washington, DC

Alabama
Birmingham Post–Herald
2200 4th Avenue
P.O. Box 2253
Birmingham, AL 35202
(205) 325-2222

Alaska
Anchorage Daily News
1001 Northway Drive
P.O. Box 149001
Anchorage, AK 99514-9001
(907) 257-4200

Arizona
The Arizona Republic
200 E. Van Buren Street
P.O. Box 2243
Phoenix, AZ 85001
(602) 271-8000

Arkansas
Arkansas Democrat–Gazette
Capitol Avenue & Scott
P.O. Box 2221
Little Rock, AR 72201
(501) 378-3400

California
Los Angeles Times
Times Mirror Square
Los Angeles, CA 90053
(213) 237-5000

Colorado
The Denver Post
1560 Broadway
Denver, CO 80202
(303) 820-1010

Connecticut
The Hartford Courant
285 Broad Street
Hartford, CT 06115-2510
(860) 241-6200

Delaware
The News Journal
950 W. Basin Road
P.O. Box 15505
Wilmington, DE 19850
(302) 324-2500

District of Columbia
The Washington Post
1150 15th Street, N.W.
Washington, DC 20071
(202) 334-6000

Florida
The Miami Herald
One Herald Plaza
Miami, FL 33132-1693
(305) 350-2111

Georgia
The Atlanta Journal–Constitution
72 Marietta Street
Atlanta, GA 30303
(404) 526-5151

Hawaii
The Honolulu Star Bulletin
    & Advertiser
605 Kapiolani Boulevard
Honolulu, HI 96813
(808) 525-8000

Idaho
The Idaho Statesman
1200 N. Curtis Road
P.O. Box 40
Boise, ID 83703
(208) 377-6200

Illinois
Chicago Sun–Times
401 N. Wabash Avenue
Chicago, IL 60611
(312) 321-3000

Indiana
The Indianapolis Star
307 N. Pennsylvania Street
Indianapolis, IN 46204
(317) 633-1240

Iowa
The Des Moines Register
715 Locust Street
P.O. Box 957
Des Moines, IA 50304
(515) 284-8000

Kansas
Wichita Eagle
825 E. Douglas Avenue
P.O. Box 820
Wichita, KS 67201-0820
(316) 268-6000

Kentucky

The Courier–Journal
P.O. Box 740031
525 W. Broadway
Louisville, KY 40201-7431
(502) 582-4011

Louisiana

The Advocate
525 Lafayette Street
Baton Rouge, LA 70802
(504) 383-1111

Maine

Bangor Daily News
491 Main Street
P.O. Box 1329
Bangor, ME 04402-1329
(207) 990-8000

Maryland

The Sun
501 N. Calvert Street
Baltimore, MD 21278
(401) 332-6000

Massachusetts

The Boston Globe
135 Morrissey Boulevard
Boston, MA 02107
(617) 929-2000

Michigan

The Detroit News and Free Press
615 W. Lafayette Boulevard
Detroit, MI 48226
(313) 222-2300

Minnesota

Star Tribune
425 Portland Avenue
Minneapolis, MN 55488
(612) 673-4000

Mississippi

The Clarion Ledger
201 S. Congress Street
P.O. Box 40
Jackson, MS 39205
(601) 961-7000

Missouri

St. Louis Post Dispatch
900 N. Tucker Boulevard
St. Louis, MO 63101
(314) 340-8000

Montana

Billings Gazette
401 N. Broadway
Billings, MT 59101
(406) 657-1200

Nebraska

Omaha World–Herald
World–Herald Square
Omaha, NE 68102
(402) 444-1000

Nevada

Las Vegas Review–Journal & Las
  Vegas Sun
1111 W. Bonanza
P.O. Box 70
Las Vegas, NV 89125-0070
(702) 383-0211

New Hampshire

The Union Leader & New
  Hampshire Sunday News
100 William Loeb Drive
Manchester, NH 03109
(603) 668-4321

New Jersey
Newark Star–Ledger
One Star–Ledger Plaza
Newark, NJ 07102-1200
(201) 877-4141

New Mexico
The Albuquerque Journal
7777 Jefferson N.E.
Albuquerque, NM 87103
(505) 823-7777

New York
New York Times
229 E. 43rd Street
New York, NY 10036
(212) 556-1234

North Carolina
The Charlotte Observer
600 S. Tyron Street
P.O. Box 32188
Charlotte, NC 28232
(704) 358-5000

North Dakota
The Forum
101 5th Street
Box 2020
Fargo, ND 58107
(701) 235-7311

Ohio
The Plain Dealer
1801 Superior Avenue
Cleveland, OH 44114
(216) 999-4500

Oklahoma
The Daily/Sunday Oklahoman
9000 N. Broadway
P.O. Box 25125
Oklahoma City, OK 73125
(405) 475-3311

Oregon
The Oregonian
1320 S.W. Broadway
Portland, OR 97201
(503) 221-8327

Pennsylvania
Pittsburgh Post–Gazette
34 Boulevard of Allies
Pittsburgh, PA 15222
(412) 263-1100

Rhode Island
The Providence Journal–Bulletin
  & The Providence Sunday
  Journal
75 Fountain Street
Providence, RI 02902
(401) 277-7000

South Carolina
The Post and Courier
Charleston News & Courier
134 Columbus Street
Charleston, SC 29403-4800
(803) 577-7111

South Dakota
Argus Leader
200 S. Minnesota Avenue
Sioux Falls, SD 57102
(605) 331-2200

Tennessee
The Tennessean
1100 Broadway
Nashville, TN 37203
(615) 259-8000

Texas
The Dallas Morning News
P.O. Box 655237
Dallas, TX 75265
(214) 977-8222

Utah
The Salt Lake Tribune
400 Tribune Building
Salt Lake City, UT 84111
(801) 237-2031

Vermont
The Burlington Free Press
191 College Street
P.O. Box 10
Burlington, VT 05401
(802) 863-3441

Virginia
The Virginian–Pilot
150 W. Brambleton Avenue
Norfolk, VA 23510
(804) 446-2000

Washington
The Seattle Times/Seattle
    Post–Intelligencer
Fairview Avenue N. & John
P.O. Box 70
Seattle, WA 98111
(206) 464-2111

West Virginia
The Charleston Gazette/Sunday
    Gazette–Mail
1001 Virginia Street E.
Charleston, WV 25301
(304) 348-5140

Wisconsin
The Milwaukee Journal Sentinel
333 W. State Street
P.O. Box 661
Milwaukee, WI 53201-0661
(414) 224-2000

Wyoming
Star–Tribune
170 Star Lane
P.O. Box 80
Casper, WY 82602
(307) 266-0500

Index

From peasant girls to Bangkok masseus